FROM THE SHADOWS

A Journey of Self-Discovery and Renewal

Elizabeth Onyeabor

For Dougard Karen

[signature]

Book cover design by Debbie O'Byrne, Denise Cassino,
and Elizabeth Onyeabor

Editing by Eye Comb Editors (www.eyecombeditors.com),
RMJ Manuscript Service LLC (www.rogenamitchell.com),
and Sojourn Publishing, LLC

Achara Bambus Creative Works, LLC

Elizabeth Onyeabor books are available for order through
Amazon.com

Visit my website: www.elizabethonyeabor.com
Follow me on Twitter: EFOnyeabor
Connect with me on Facebook: ElizabethOnyeaborAuthor

Printed in the United States of America
First Printing: October 2016
Publisher: Sojourn Publishing, LLC

ISBN-10: 1627472320
ISBN-13: 978-1627472326

DEDICATION

To my beloved friends and family:

You loved me when I did not love myself.

Thank you for your compassionate companionship.

CONTENTS

INTRODUCTION

Welcome to my tale of transformation. Unwinding depression is not a neat process, but I guide you along my path as I walked it. Most of all, I offer you hope. As tormented and hopeless as I was, I am now healed.

You can heal, too.

You will discover what I uncovered about myself in the way it progressed for me. My journey was not chronologically linear. Neither is this book. I describe my struggle from 2012 to 2015, weaving intensity with insight.

To paraphrase a sentiment, if all the world's a stage and our lives are plays, we compare our rough rehearsals to others' polished performances. Through vignettes and verse, I draw back my curtain to spotlight backstage feelings, thoughts, and perspectives. I reenact adulthood and childhood sketches from memory and notes.

I share journal excerpts. Although condensed and corrected for clarity, these private thoughts are otherwise unedited, never imagining future publication. In the depths of my anguish, I use a few expletives. Thank you for understanding.

Discretion directs me to keep confidential certain actions from behind-the-scenes. However, I show you how I processed them so they no longer shroud me in guilt and shame. I also change a few names and other details to maintain privacy or anonymity.

After the epilogue, I include a section summarizing key points, offering suggestions, and posing questions for you to contemplate on your own journey of self-discovery. Also, consider writing down how you feel whenever a part of my story triggers deep emotion. Answer any questions I posed to myself that also resonate with you. Most importantly, write how you feel, however you feel. Writing about emotions is a cathartic, healing release.

As you expose wounds so they finally begin to heal, don't try to mend everything by yourself. You will need other people's resources and support. Go to the people you feel safe with. There may be different people for different issues. There are also support groups and crisis centers in many countries (worldwide listings are available at sites such as www.iasp.info). Perhaps there are resources where you live. Maybe you will start a support group yourself.

If you feel overwhelmed or suicidal, reach out to a prevention hotline, crisis center, coach, counselor, therapist, or someone you love for help.

You are already enough. One day, you will know this, too.

DESCENT INTO DESPAIR

I feel like I can't keep happiness down.

I keep vomiting it back up...

1
PROLOGUE

The story of how my soul nearly died...

When I Am Gone

When I am gone
only those who loved
will remember
and cherish the memory
when I am gone

No more will I be
ruminating about past failures
No more will I be
fearing a disappointing future
And no more will I be
at all
except in remembrance

Some would say
I will be
in perfectness too
but no one

can say for sure
that there will be
anything at all

It is belief disguised as certainty
in some sort of life hereafter
I am under no such illusion
And no more will I be
when I am gone

࿔ **2015** ࿔

I rest in the circle of light in the crimson sandstone cavern of my thoughts. The warm, radiant beams are invigorating to my body and soul. I want them to wash over me and give me the inspiration that I know brims within. In this brilliant cave of my thought, I feel the sparkling rays twirl over me, giving my soul the opportunity to dance in the radiance after my long, gloomy period of darkness—one from which I believed I never wanted to leave alive. This light-and-dark dance entwining within me is what I tell you about now.

Maybe it resonates with the light and dark reverberating in your own soul. For me, it just is, and I can't contain it in only my mind any longer. My heart guides me to share this painful journey. My eyes well with the tears I weep in joy and sorrow as I tell you the story of how my soul nearly died.

࿔࿔

I had many nicknames in my childhood, from Betsy Wetsy to Betsy Boo, but most especially, Beth. That was the name of my older sisters' favorite character in *Little Women*. Shortly after I arrived home from the hospital, a candy contest settled my name.

Dad was nearly forty-nine, with a thick, white shock of slightly wavy hair slicked back to reveal his age-deepened hairline.

His white hair was a handsome complement to his ruddy, freckled face, a result of decades of outdoor construction work. With two or three strikes of the hammer, Dad's large and heavily freckled hands could expertly set and pound a nail into a two-by-four.

Dad offered my brother Quintin a choice. Quintin, with his wavy, dark brown hair and the same blue-green eyes I inherited, was nearly three years old, but my name's fate rested in his and Dad's hands. A piece of candy crinkled in each of Dad's outstretched palms, its citrus tang mixing with his sweet sawdust scent. One candy represented Carol, a name Dad liked. It was also the name of his teen crush. Mom was not enthusiastic about that association. With her Greta Garbo eyes and tall, trim model stature, Mom was a brunette beauty. She had nothing to fear from Carol's vestiges. The other hand represented Elizabeth, my paternal grandmother's name. Luckily, for Mom and my sisters, Quintin plucked the palm for Elizabeth. My family usually called me Beth.

In my mind's eye, Beth was a sweet soul with dark brown hair and a slightly pudgy tummy in an otherwise trim body. She also felt picked on. Quintin, always adventurous and active, loved her so much, he would play with her all the time, but his antics would eventually end in Beth's crying.

As a teenager, Beth shifted her persona. She refused to answer to her childhood nickname and insisted on another. She cut short her nearly waist-length brown hair. She shifted to pragmatic. Liz was born.

That is the backdrop, but there's much more to this story. Let's fast forward to almost the present day. Liz wrestles with the feelings she doesn't want to feel, the anger she hasn't been acknowledging, and a fixated desperation about how she wants her husband and adult children to change. She seeks solace in her journal.

Excerpt One

I don't know why this incredible sadness envelops me. I know that it happens when I feel powerless, events around me seem so out of whack with my desires, and I'm emotionally exhausted. I compare it to when I had food poisoning. I feel like I can't keep happiness down. I keep vomiting it back up.

She had disconnected two parts of herself. Her feelings side was stuck in her discarded Beth identity, while Liz was logical, like *Star Trek*'s fictional Spock from the planet Vulcan. This is the story of her awakening. When she connected the heart of Beth with the head of Liz, she became whole again and healed as Elizabeth.

I'll tell you about the worst pain first.

2
HOPELESS HOLE

The hopelessness is an immeasurable burden

burrowing a black hole through me, swallowing all my light...

ᘓ **2012** ᘔ

I collapse and curl into a ball on the cold, hard, stained concrete floor. Howling, I release all hope.

The brown, cream, and tan stippled floor is the work of my labor to stain and lacquer every bit of it. I'm proud of my effort. It's meaningless in this moment. It's simply the place for me to wail in the kitchen where my family is not getting along. I cannot see how anything, after all these years, is going to change.

I can only feel the depth of hope evaporating from my body like a lake vanishing into the desert of hopelessness. I am riddled with guilt and shame, and I can't shake it no matter how much my family tells me they love me.

I am in the deepest part of my depression. An incident is triggering me: a family argument. The topics change, yet now the emotion hits harder. My Liz armor of so many decades isn't there anymore. I don't know how to be Beth. How to feel is overwhelming.

The molten fire raging within erupts, and I explode. My screeches pierce the atmosphere like a blonde banshee. I can't contain the anguish. I sob as my chest heaves in spastic bellows, and I really don't care that they hear. Okay, actually I do. I *want* them to see the agony, in a physical manifestation, that I'm going through. I can't articulate it because there are no words, and I'm feeling so helpless and can't utter anything. I'm not yelling—just shrieking and sobbing.

I don't remember how I got into the bedroom. I do remember thinking, "I can't take this anymore—the torment is too much. I want to sleep forever."

I search the internet and land on a page describing many ways to end the misery. It also tells me how many people are unsuccessful at how they try, and the aftereffects.

See, Liz, logical Liz, is a Vulcan. She wants it to be clean and unfeeling. Really, isn't that the point? To not feel? So why would she want to die while suffering? Sleep. Numb. Painless. No feeling. Yeah, that's what Liz wants.

The website describes the author's own struggles. I feel a kindred spirit of a sort and read each trial, thinking I couldn't attempt suicide those ways. I'm too chicken. I marvel at his efforts to end his agony.

I want to end *my* agony. I don't have any easy, ready mechanisms available. I want to be sure. I keep reading. I'm a little bit frightened about the list of aftereffects. If I'm going to fail, then I don't want to be disabled for the rest of my life, however long that might be. I'm not sure what to do.

My daughter Victoria, mortified, musters all the wisdom offered by her twenty-eight years and pries me away from the website. Now listless, I am prostrate on the bed, wrapped in red and black coverings. I hear comforting words and encouragement, but it doesn't stick. How can I take any action when I feel so incapable and in such a quagmire? Volunteer? Help other people? I don't have any energy for that. Might as well tell me to train to be an astronaut and fly to the moon. It feels just that impossible at the moment. I don't tell Victoria that. I don't have that defined thought then. I see the concern in her beautiful, dark-brown eyes. Her long, black ringlets air bounce as she leans forward, perched at the bed's edge, trying to console and cheer me. I know whatever she's encouraging me to do right now, it is not going to work. I can't do it.

I can only lie here. The salty tears wet my red and black pillow. It's as if the weeping has turned on a leaky faucet, because anytime I blink, and even when I don't, they well up and begin to roll down the side of my face. I see no point in wiping them away. More will come.

I hear words of love, but it only intensifies unworthiness. More tears well. My chest constricts, my breathing shallows, and my jaw clenches, grinding my teeth together. I don't consciously realize any of this. I'm only wondering if the hurt will ever go away on this horrible roller-coaster ride of emotions. It's crushing.

I want comatose oblivion. If my mind wills it, will my body follow? It is a secret, desperate wish. If I can do it by myself, there won't be medical complications like with drugs. I lie there until, somehow, sleep comes, and I have some respite.

I awake to hear something in the hallway. Is that the sound of pleasant voices? The family members so recently feuding are hugging. Can this be? A feeble ray of hope flickers through the ashy atmosphere. Is there, really, hope?

My family seems to reconcile. I sense the soft click as my imaginary cart engages and ascends the track. My spirits lift. I suspend the internet search for my end.

This is my roller coaster. Other people are controlling my feelings. I react. I don't choose my response. It's automatic, not conscious. No wonder I feel so horrible. I have no control, and I'm riding in emotion land. I have no steering wheel.

ᮗᏯᏣᎧ

We begin a road trip to the neighboring state for a family reunion with my siblings and their families. I take my turn driving. Or, am I driving? I'm not there most of the time. Logical Liz is an experienced driver so she can do it well.

Beth, however, feels mired in the muck as her grip tightens around the wheel. Her knuckles whiten, eyes glaze, and face distorts, provoking her adult children into a panic. She's veering into a bottomless whirlpool. It draws her in as she paints a putrid past of what a terrible mother she is. She knows it. She knows this because all the stories replaying in her head are like a horror movie, starring her. They show failure after failure. The family helps steer her clear and then unseats her. From the passenger seat, she perceives their gentle coaxing. Her riptide ebbs as she drifts back to their protection for the remainder of the six-hour drive.

My three older sisters, Kathleen, Kristine, and Yvonne, are already there. Kathleen is the oldest, followed by Kristine, then Yvonne. Kathleen's wavy, light-blonde hair is just shy of shoulder length. Kris is the only brunette now. Kris keeps her brown tufts cut short and sassy. Yvonne has always been blonde, and she keeps her straight, golden locks in a shoulder-length bob. I have a headache and need to buy some pain reliever. Kristine drives me to the grocery store. I am pretending everything is fine, but I cannot keep up this façade much longer.

In aisle number nine, I finally blurt out, "I'm suicidal."

Kristine gives me a big hug, telling me how much she loves me, and she knows how I feel. I know she cares. Then she tells me part of her own struggle with depression and remedies. At our shared height, my blue-green eyes look into her ocean-blue eyes. We see past our physical windows and gaze into each other's spirits. We connect our core essences at that moment. We are two souls who don't feel good enough.

My torment is still there although I feel a little less crazy than the instant before.

I recall some family members have struggled with depression; it had never sunk in before. It wasn't my problem. Well, that's what I thought at the time. I didn't recognize my problem. I had never been suicidal before.

Kristine and I finish our shopping and talk some more. She gathers Kathleen and Yvonne together, and I share my anguish. They reveal theirs. They share other stories about close and extended family members and their struggles. I talk to another relative who shares his battle with depression and his remedies, including prescription medication.

I am finding solace knowing I'm not the only one. My distress is so great that I divulge many details I would not typically unveil.

My husband Gillis and my children join us. Gillis takes my lightly freckled hand in his own strong, dark hands to comfort me. We brainstorm possible actions. I hope they will work for me. I'm tired of feeling this way. It's painful for Gillis and my kids. They all want me to feel better.

They aren't used to seeing me vulnerable. They aren't used to seeing me so incredibly sad. Hmm, that's not the right word. I admit, when I hear people describe depression, they talk about sadness. There is sadness, but it's so much more. It's *hopelessness*.

The hopelessness is an immeasurable burden burrowing a black hole through me, swallowing all my light. Hope itself taunts me and spits in my face as it evaporates, leaving me isolated in darkness.

I know my emotions are dependent on others. External events trigger me. A feeling of powerlessness makes me believe there is nothing I can do about it. There will be no miracle to take the torture away, ever.

That's the thing. It is beyond sadness. At least that's how it was for me. You or someone you love may feel it differently. Depression is a powerful feeling of dis-ease.

It has also not been easy to open up about this. It's kind of taboo. Like saying, "Hey, I have a secret shame. I'm really an alien. You should think I'm weird." That's a bit how it feels.

Also, there's the labeling. I have relatives who may not want to be associated with someone coming out of the closet of depression. Actually, it's not a closet. It's a whirlpool. It's a quagmire. It's like slogging through sinking sand while the black hole saps the hope.

Not So Secretly Sad

"Are you secretly sad?"
The website queried.
Not so secretly,
Not so publicly,
Yes, so sad.

It was a secret
I kept to myself.
Thinking somehow crazed
I must be.

Knowing it was not
a normal thing to feel.
Not managing to
embrace or savor
joy for any length—
evaporated like spirits.

Couldn't describe
what I was hiding.
Sobbing alone
even when my sweetie
was in the very next room.

Revealing my burden
felt less heavy
but didn't release it.
Sorrow persisted as
heart and head arrhythmia.

Failure. Rumination. Speculation.
Compliments like arrows
pierced my mask and
lodged deep inside.
Didn't deserve them,
didn't they know?

Loved ones empathetic,
bear their own distress.
Yes, they have secretly
also been sad.
Not so secretly.
Not so publicly.
No, not so sad now.

Takes effort and desire
sometimes just to
leave the bed
let alone get ahead.
Shift my thoughts
then my feelings.

Not so secret.
Not so public.
Still at times sad.
Yet at times happy too.
Express and don't suppress
to feel more at balance.

Sharing with my siblings was a release. We talked at length about my depression. They encouraged my kids and Gillis in ways to support me.

Because another family member had received relief through antidepressant medication, I was hoping for the same result. I talked to a doctor and filled a prescription to take with me to Lagos. I had returned to the US on vacation to visit family and friends. This was my first trip back since moving to Nigeria two years earlier.

I read research about antidepressants; they are not always successful and carry significant risks. Studies also stated they take a while before kicking in their magic when they do work.

I thought about alternatives. For example, I could exercise for endorphins, but that also felt like going to the moon most of the time; it seemed impossible to get regular motivation for exercise. I'd already tried that. I needed something easier.

I investigated natural approaches as an alternative. I found an herb some studies had reported as helpful. On my return to Lagos, I carried both the prescription antidepressant drugs and herbal tablets with me.

I took the natural medicine first. I was keeping the prescription antidepressants on hand in case I didn't feel the desired results from the herbal tablets. After a few weeks, I decided the herbal medicine was helping, even if it might have been a placebo effect. I never took any prescription medication, but I continued the natural remedy for a year.

Silicon sea
Sucks me
Inwardly

Struggle
Sink
Stress

Feel so dire
In quagmire

Anxiety

ᏸᎧᏣ

Before I vacationed in the US, I had spent a few months replaying scathing scenes from my past. I sobbed in solitary, randomly wrote in my journal, and sought sympathy from my best friends, Katharina and Layla, before I admitted to Gillis and my kids that I felt crazy—crazy like I had never felt before.

I had felt sad, even depressed before. This feeling was far beyond those. As a teenager, I had said many times that I never understood why someone would want to commit suicide. Now, I totally understood. And everyone could judge me for feeling that way, too. Admitting that weakness and vulnerability felt like I had flaws not acceptable to society.

When I first told Gillis how I was feeling, he didn't know how to react. He was driving in Lagos's commuter traffic. Exhaust fume stench filled the air. Impatient taxi drivers hollered with their honks as they crammed and cut queues. His dark-brown eyes stared intently ahead, concentrating on maneuvering through ten merging lanes approaching the Lekki tollbooth. I looked at the soft curves of his silhouette and the kinky black-and-gray curls shorn so close they seemed straight. It wasn't good timing, but I couldn't stop myself.

I said, "I think I'm going crazy."

Then I went into details about my depressing thoughts. He wanted to take action, tell me what to do, tell me how to snap out of it. He was full of good intentions, but it made me feel like he didn't understand. It was a relief to tell him, though.

I couldn't snap out of it. I was still dependent on others. I was unconsciously reactive, not consciously responding. These did not feel like my own choices. I kept waiting for circumstances to shift so they could alter the way I was feeling. It was other people's fault—*and* I was responsible for everything—simultaneously.

It sounds odd when I write it, yet the feeling was just that. I was responsible for failing to maintain family harmony among Gillis, Victoria, Kenneth, Christopher, and myself. The ideal in my head superimposed itself over all the actions and interactions. Yes, they should conform to my image of the happy, functional family. I wanted it so much, and I shouldered the bulk of the blame.

I thought, "If only I had done this or that…" Really, I got to the point where I concluded that because I didn't do X, Y, or Z, then I was a failure as a mother. Everything was solely and squarely in my camp. It was not in my mind that it was not realistic. Emotions have nothing to do with logic.

As Liz, I had disconnected from Beth. I shut off Beth along with damming the emotions she embodied. I'd closeted her in a cave since I was a teenager—well, except now and then in moments of extreme feeling that I couldn't contain. So, there I was, hoping my family members would change and interact with each other differently, and at the same time shouldering the blame for why it wasn't working in the way I wanted it to—my own maternal failure.

Shift from the Middle

Shift from the middle,
between polarities,
well, really, personalities—
from mutual unease.

Perhaps it sounds like my family was a mess. In your eyes, we might be. In others' eyes, we might look great. Most don't know what we don't tell, and this isn't an exposé about Gillis, Victoria, Kenneth, or Christopher. This is only my perspective. I had unmet expectations.

I believed I had not acted as I should have. It didn't matter that my views were not realistic. It didn't matter that many families had problems the same as or worse than ours. I can only tell you the way I felt. I looked back on nearly three decades of our history together, and I painted all of it as a Rembrandt, not a Monet.

Monet-like images with flowers and light splotches of vibrant colors existed, of course, but my mind had dark grays, dull browns, and depressing blacks of a Rembrandt self-portrait. There wasn't joy in my imagery. Just as oil colors can paint over each other, my mind had camouflaged my history with these frightening feelings of darkness and despair.

Why did I select the Rembrandt reference? Two unique oil paintings hung in my childhood home—one of each grandmother I never knew. One died before my birth, and the other died when I was still toddling around unsteadily.

My maternal grandmother, Mary, has a beautiful pink, large-brimmed hat. A large ostrich feather adorns it. She is wearing a white blouse and has twinkling, sky-blue eyes, with a faint smile, exuding kindness. Mary's portrait always made me feel good to look at her.

Elizabeth, my paternal grandmother, is wearing a black blouse. Her tanned face shows the wrinkles of her age. Elizabeth's hair has faint streaks of gray but is otherwise jet black, fading into the darkness of the canvas's background. Her eyes are as dark as her blouse, projecting harshness. I was afraid of Elizabeth's rendering when I was young.

I asked the portrait artist why the paintings were so contrasting. She had attempted a Rembrandt-like theme for Elizabeth. Later, she realized some of her suppressed emotion about the challenges she faced with Elizabeth, as her mother-in-law, found expression in her depiction. The artist was my mother.

Apparently, suppressing emotions is not a new thing in our family. Open expression was only encouraged when acting as other characters in community theater. Expression of emotion finds various ways to come out eventually, though. Like water, it always finds a way. When my emotions surfaced, they burst a dam. The gushing lake flooded me.

When engulfed, I didn't feel like going out. Going to work was enough. Besides, I couldn't easily navigate the bustling Lagos metropolis with millions of crazy drivers. Strike that. Let's call them erratic drivers. Remember, I was the crazy one.

What were some helpful activities? I wrote. I read. I downloaded books on my computer and read the e-versions. I didn't finish some books. In other books, I highlighted key points. I read books about meaning, ancient philosophy, emotional intelligence, and boundaries. I read a lot.

One of the books I read, *The Artist's Way* by Julia Cameron (Tarcher Books, 1992), instructed me to write every morning. I tried for a while, but I like the evenings better. Mornings have never been my thing unless they're the wee hours of the morning.

In any event, I followed the exercises each morning, scrawling my prescribed number of pages longhand. I obediently wrote each morning as soon as I woke up. Gillis would beckon me to come back to our cozy bed. Instead, I would write until the page quotas were completed. One day, feeling particularly rejected, Gillis challenged my writing.

"You're not going to change on me, quit your job, and become a writer, are you?"

I laughed and snorted, "Don't be ridiculous. That would be crazy. I'm just doing this to see if it helps."

I described feelings and random thoughts entering my head. I also wrote some intuitive blurts in those exercises. They only made sense to me a few years later when I re-read them. After a few months, I stopped. I was prefacing them "to my wonderful self," and I didn't feel wonderful. I was a fraud.

I wanted to know if depression had been following me for a long time, unnamed. I was on a quest to investigate the past. I began reading my teenage journals.

My journals described many activities with friends, then feelings of emptiness when I was alone. I had spent my teenage years keeping busy doing school work, acting in plays with family members, doing activities with friends, longing for a boyfriend to complete me, and feeling empty when I was alone. See a pattern? Busyness. Emptiness. Sadness. Depression. My teenage depression was not deep yet. It was not at a crisis point. It was already present, though.

I had been sad and depressed, and I didn't know it. I didn't access or allow myself to feel pain. I didn't acknowledge emotions were there unless they spawned overpowering torment. I usually successfully distracted myself with activities or busyness. I took seven classes per semester instead of the usual six. I didn't stay in the dam of Beth's emotions long. Logical Liz rescued me with other activities.

Now, I had identified there was a history. A part of the equation I had solved. Some siblings suffered depression. A part of the mystery I had unraveled. I hadn't cured my quandary, though. I still needed to go further.

I was keeping busy at times while trying to solve my own depressing problems, but it was like fixing a broken wheel on a moving car. I didn't want to stop the momentum, though my car was tilting to the side, listing in one direction, and getting stuck in pothole after pothole. I was pushing and not driving. It was exhausting.

During my major depressive episodes, I still went to work. I know some people are so affected that they can barely function, but my professional mask was so secure, it enabled me to go to work. Work was easy if it kept me busy. Solving problems there was less emotional. Busyness was a great escape. Busyness or business didn't require me to feel my own horrible thoughts. I could distract myself.

On most weekends, I would sleep thirteen hours or more. Some days, I would come home from work, quickly eat, and then crawl into bed, hoping the emptiness would go away.

That's the other thing about my depression. The hopeless hole was insatiable. Sometimes it would be stronger than at other times, like a hungry animal devouring the joy of the last few hours until the misery is all that's left.

Reading my story, you might have intense emotions—whether you want to acknowledge them or not. The quagmire may be sucking you in. It's okay. I'll lighten up for a little while. It used to pull me in mercilessly, too. I get it.

ƧƆ

There were a few bright spots among my dark periods. I journaled I wanted to feel bliss and be present in the moment. Sometimes, my wish came true.

Excerpt Two

It was about forty-five minutes to one hour by boat. On the way back, I felt so in the moment—perfectly peaceful and happy. Wishing I could feel like that always.

The area we traveled through is a natural lake that extends between the strip of land bordering the sea and the mainland. So much unspoiled beauty in coconut and palm trees. The wind raced against my face, cooling my touch of sunburn.

I felt like a dog peering over the boat's windshield as the sun set behind us. Maybe it was the nature. Maybe it was the few glasses of wine. Maybe it was both. I want to fully embrace and capture that moment of pure, lasting pleasure.

Bliss

The sun hangs low in the sky,
Faint spray of water mists the bow,
Wind rushing past me and my guy.

I don't know why or how,
In this moment,
I embrace the present;
I feel bliss.

The past is not haunting,
Nor the future daunting.
In this moment,
Is only the present.

I drink the air deeply and hold
Onto this standstill in time.
Rays kiss from the orb of gold,
Nature's gift so sublime.

In this moment,
I have a present.
I feel bliss.

I wanted to hold the feeling. Throughout this period, I searched for articles online in addition to the books I read. I diligently took my herbal medicine and exercised when I could. The exercise and the self-help were both sporadic.

I thought of sessions with a US-based therapist, but unless I had been an established patient, the practitioners I contacted would not treat me as a long-distance patient. Perhaps I didn't search hard enough. I didn't find anyone. My energy levels were low, so when I met obstacles, I didn't vigorously pursue.

I also didn't have a social network of friends in Lagos. I had moved there several months before I hit rock bottom and occasionally socialized with work acquaintances. I attended a couple of women's groups composed of Americans and other foreigners.

However, in my despair, I didn't feel like socializing as I normally would. The effort required in establishing friendships felt crushing. I was often in an unenjoyable state. Attending women's group meetings was a nice distraction, but afterward, the emptiness would come gnawing back.

Though I felt sad, hopeless, and empty, one of the first emotions I explored was anger.

3
ANGRY
ACKNOWLEDGMENT

Good people don't express anger...

During my visit to the US, Christopher took me aside. He desperately wanted to help me feel better and had done some research on his own. I gazed on his long, angular jaw that reminds me of my brothers, Steven and Quintin, and his deep-caramel complexion. His soft brown eyes showed loving concern as he shared with me that he had read somewhere, "Depression is suppressed anger turned inward."

He suggested I take some paper and start with the phrase, "What I am most angry about is..." It sounded a bit far-fetched to me. I wasn't mad. I was sad. I was a failure. That was my fixation.

I was wrong. I *was* actually angry, too.

I tried Christopher's suggestion, after my initial resistance. I wrote non-stop, a stream of consciousness type of writing, for more than an hour, on five pages of a large-lined notebook. My rage and resentment spanned decades. It was stunning. I surprised myself. Maybe there was something to this anger-repression-depression connection.

In most cases, what I was mad about were things I couldn't change and had a profound impact on my life. The most distressing issue was a car crash from 1984 disabling Gillis and preventing him from working for several years. It surprised me to see it surface on my livid missive.

My feelings about the mishap were hanging around in the recesses of my mind. I didn't blame the other driver for the collision itself—that's why we call them *accidents*. The domino effect of medical issues, finances, and impact on Gillis's well-being and our family situation made me upset. Writing this even now, I feel my jaw tighten and my teeth clench. It was a hard time after he had the car accident.

Here are a couple of selections from my anger epistle.

Excerpt Three

What I am most angry about is that I have a shitty life, filled with so much drama in my family that never seems to end. I'm angry with myself for not being able to fix it since I can fix nearly everything else and have a sense of accomplishment. I'm a problem solver, and I have not been able to solve this problem...

I am angry that we had that stupid accident so many years ago. That changed how my life was to be—forever! I thought I would be able to be a mother staying at home taking care of my kids, and that Ann bitch hit the car and injured Gillis, and I had to work for the rest of my life.

That is the most significant event that has happened to me, and it didn't happen directly to me. I'm now surprised, in a way, that this is coming up, but it makes sense that I have anger at my circumstances, the perpetrator of which is a faceless entity that I can't even hold in contempt.

> Sure, it was an accident, so I can't really blame her for it...The accident happened to Gillis, and I really couldn't ever get angry about it because he was so angry and I had to support him. It didn't happen to me, but it felt like it happened to me, and nothing was ever the same.

My friend Katharina has access to tools for personal development. She offered to let me take an assessment of my emotional intelligence, covering several dimensions. One of the factors was my access to anger. My result was the lowest she had ever seen.

I was in the top one percentile on the repression-of-anger scale compared to everyone else who had ever taken the assessment. I was not accessing my anger. I was not allowing myself to feel it. It doesn't mean anger wasn't there. It means I didn't *acknowledge* anger.

The question I asked myself was, "Why didn't I think or feel that anger was something I should access or express?" I thought about my history and realized there were several reasons.

In my childhood family—what the books call the family of origin—there was a general suppression of emotions. My parents rarely argued by the time I was born. They had been married for fourteen years by then. Suppression had become an art form in my family, and that included anger.

We pattern the models we see. My conditioned belief was that good people don't express anger. I also believed demonstrating indignation and disagreement were not healthy and natural but something to hide. I had mistakenly interpreted that concealing vexations was a way of expressing love.

I realized I subscribed to the myths that someone else made me feel angry and through their behavior, someone else should fix how I was feeling. I also believed expressing my displeasure to a person dear to me would put the relationship at risk.

I get teary and cry when I finally do express anger. It's a big deal for me. Because I cry, it makes me feel as though I look weak and vulnerable, and it lessens the impact of my outrage. I am angry that I cry when I'm angry.

Gillis freely expresses his ire. It makes sense that I would instinctively find that trait attractive and simultaneously distressing. The result was I didn't have to express anger most of the time. Gillis did it for both of us. I could go on suppressing it. These weren't conscious thoughts, mind you. I see this in retrospect. I couldn't see them as they were happening.

Not Sure Why

Not sure why
just turn my head
and cry at times

Could be a commercial
could be an emotional
part of a movie
where the loved one
breaks down in grief

Could be when I write
my deepest feelings
though I write of joy too

It is the pain that
like a sword into its scabbard
plunges deep
firm
and swift
impaling
all
breath

I am stabbed by
the emotion the author
filmmaker or director
evoked in me stoked in me
that was already there
somewhere

Wonder why joy rarely
overcomes so swiftly
suddenly and completely?

Or perhaps it does
disguised as a laugh
that overtakes to the
point of breathlessness

In both cases my chest heaves
my facial expression's extreme
completely engrossed in
the moment

Even a hearty laugh
can sound like a sob
from a distance

To seem so close
but feel so differently
Not sure why

ৰ০৫৪

I don't blame anyone for my depression now. I take responsibility. I want to provide context. I am beginning to understand how to be a balanced and authentic self. This needs to come with getting at root causes so I can unwind them. I don't blame my parents for suppressing their feelings. I don't blame their parents either. I expect this has been going on for generations.

However, in the depths of my depression, I had no compassion for myself. I blamed myself for not doing, knowing, or being aware of my issues. I simply wasn't ready to deal with them then. I see that now.

If you are feeling this way, please have some compassion for yourself.

My anger manifested as passive-aggressive behavior because I suppressed it and did not express it overtly. Passive-aggression is not transparent. I became good at secrets. It became part of my job to deal with various company secrets. I dealt with inappropriate employee behavior investigations, corporate reorganizations, and downsizings. I was good at keeping those close to my vest. No wonder—I'd had a lot of practice in other ways.

How have I done now with my anger? I know now its gift is that it provides cues about infringed boundaries. It also motivates us to act. I wasn't aware of those signals at the time. I would process my indignation later, when I processed it at all, after it had built up.

I know I can express outrage through venting and healthily combine it with compassion. I can also mindfully hold it inwardly, acknowledging it's there when it is not yet appropriate to express.

Lately, I have done a better job of voicing it. The key is that I'm now aware. I express and choose the timing and method of expression. I've written angry notes I never delivered. Yet, writing the notes helped with clarity in understanding the anger at myself that I projected onto others when I allowed them to trample or pass through my unenforced emotional boundaries.

Since I was the one who didn't enforce them, how could they know? There was no marker stating "Danger. Don't pass my emotional boundary." Formerly, I would acquiesce and say nothing. Now, I am saying them on the spot or soon after. I'm writing about concerns I have had a hard time articulating. It's helpful.

This is something I struggle at times to practice. Being a doormat used to seem easier than shaking off the dirt and creating a cloud of dust through showing anger. Now, I don't want muck piling up before shaking it off. It's less messy that way and easier to keep clean. Oh, I don't want to be a doormat, either.

Anger

Now you've returned.
I thought you had gone,
at least for a time,
but you probably lurked
just under the surface,
simmering quietly,
when I thought I had
expressed you,
released you.

You seem a bit thinner,
or lost some vigor,
or maybe just the rage
that made you so large
was what I released.
The skeleton remains,
like the Mummy returning
with fleshy parts attached,
not the monster I felt.

When I set my limits to
clearly define wants,
desires, and needs,
will you then leave?

To further shift my thinking and false beliefs about fury, I wrote out the following as a reminder to myself, as well as to create a new internal dialog:

> *Excerpt Four*
> All relationships can express anger, and it can be healthy, especially when it is responsibly expressed.
> Everyone feels anger at some point; it's okay.
> I make myself angry based on my reaction. It is my responsibility to express it appropriately and release it (not suppress it).
> I can use anger as an opportunity, a motivator to action, and a tool for insights about my triggers because often the anger is about a boundary I allowed to be crossed.

4
ROOTS OF RUMINATION

I felt a failure as a mother...

Secret

I have a secret hidden
It stays with me inside
Where nobody can see it
And in none else confide

Catching short my breath
Burns my solar plexus
Tightening my chest
Beckons me to anxious

A constant companion
Oft forget it's there
Till my back reminds
The weight it must bear

Little triggers spark
A flame that full ignites
Feeding on my fears
Burning orange blight

Threatens to unmask
Veil of shame, disgrace
So cleverly enshrouding
Façade before the face

Won't guess my secret
Shan't give you any clue
Can only say with certainty
You surely have one, too

You wonder details about why I was depressed. The reasons triggering me, well, they all centered on my family. I told you that much. They're not earth-shattering to anyone else, just me.

If I went into all the specifics, you might surmise they were mere molehills, but to me, they were massive mountains. I feel differently and have a changed perspective now, although many situations and patterns of interactions persist, and I cannot change anything about my past.

I felt a failure as a mother. I believed I had not provided the protective, nurturing environment I should have in so many ways. I worked throughout my children's childhood. That was something I vowed not to do. I planned to be a stay-at-home mom.

I had studied secretarial skills in high school. I planned to work until I had children, and then I intended to work only part time while they were in school. A secretarial job was something supplementary and flexible, but certainly not a career I was looking for long term.

My focus was to rear a family. That was primary. My bitterness about the car accident was Gillis's injury and incapacity. The doctors told me he would never be able to work again.

I needed to provide for my struggling family and support them financially when Gillis was suddenly incapacitated. I felt I must shoulder sole responsibility for the rest of my life. An internal lever switched on, commanding the strength of a superwoman. Like the Titan Atlas, I bore my family's balled-up burdens. I supported the family until he regained his health a few years later and resumed his career. However, the imprint of colossal responsibility to carry the family's concerns did not go away, even when Gillis became the primary provider again. Believing it to be a lifetime obligation, I continued working to feed the greed of my herculean identity.

Roller Coaster

The path I thought straight
Turns with a sudden lurch and jerk
Clacking a steady climb onward, upward
Only to descend so quickly I actually feel G-force
I scream with fright
It's only a ride
Coach says, "Wave your hands in the air
And enjoy the ride down
You'll go up in time"
It's only life

Most of all, I believed my ability to stay at home with my children, and watch them grow as I had planned, was stolen from me. I had not expressed my outrage. It had been within me for almost thirty years when I journaled my five pages of anger.

Not being a stay-at-home mom was a root cause of some of the regret and shame I felt. If only I had been around my children more, then *fill in the blank* wouldn't have happened. If only I hadn't been compelled to work, then *fill in the blank* would have happened. There were numerous things to fill in the blanks with.

I enjoyed my human resources career. I liked it so much that, at times, I let the busyness take over to fill the emptiness I may have otherwise faced. Yes, busyness was a form of workaholism. I regretted that as well.

Thirty years is a lot of remorse for someone to store up. I had numerous issues to feel guilt and shame about. It didn't matter whether or not my adult children had forgiven me, or never blamed me in the first place, for the way things were. I blamed myself enough for all of us. They didn't need to.

My lack of family utopia bothered me, and it festered the wound that my motherhood didn't work out as planned. I had suppressed anger about this, and it ran so deeply that I had hidden the original trigger from my view. I believed the suppressed anger was all about regret and wrath at myself.

Excerpt Five

I obsessively cling to the idea of a harmonious, healthy family. And yet I, in my obsession, am not even approaching it healthily. How ironic.

At times, it feels hopeless and unattainable. It has been my only purpose…So, worrying about it, obviously, doesn't help. Trying to "fix" issues disempowers others and makes it no better. I know I logically can't control it, but I feel compelled irrationally to believe there must be something I can do.

Referee

Used to play referee
in the middle for my part,
each player grabs a piece
of my heart to tear apart.

Yellow and red the
cards I would show,
play upon play,
and so it would go.

The drama unfolds,
the years they go by,
one forward one back,
with a laugh and a cry.

Now one of the players
has thrown in the towel,
accuses team members
of playing so foul.

Gone from the pitch,
full of anger and blame.
He now maneuvers
through alternative game.

Disjointed today,
no middle man needed,
was fooling myself,
since wasn't so heeded.

Team's deep chasm
seems beyond repair.
Desperate to restore,
fall prey to despair.

Injured, gone from the
field, watch plays
on diff'ring pitches,
not a referee's gaze.

Mere observer today,
but tucked in my mind...
hope one day to unite,
play together in kind.

INSPIRATIONAL INCEPTION

I'm not an artist. I just want to feel like

I'm more creative or have a creative outlet...

5
PASSIONATE PURSUITS

When I didn't allow myself to feel fury,

I couldn't sense its polar opposite—passion...

never thought I had passion. I admired people who were passionate about what they did. It was exciting to watch, observe, and encourage. Passion combined with creativity was something I most admired. I considered myself sensible and practical. I liked what I did in human resources, but I wouldn't have described it as passionate—ever.

> *Excerpt Six*
> A question. I don't know exactly what the answer is: what is my passion? I follow Gillis's dreams because I allow them to be mine. I don't have ones of my own outside of human resources, really. I know I'm about helping others maximize, but have I done that with myself?

I enjoyed discussing passions—other people's passions. I was in awe and envy when they talked about them. I sometimes wondered why I didn't feel a beautiful burning desire, but I figured some people just don't have an inspirational flame blazing in them.

Perhaps, like anger, passion was another self-proclaimed myth for me to look at differently. I explored the evolution of my professional career.

I wrote how at a young age I decided to become a nurse. I would help people, sick people, to heal. I remembered reading a book from the school library about becoming a nurse. By fourth grade, I documented my desire to be a part-time nurse and artist, but most of all I would be a mother. I planned my life; it was a perfect choice, until the summer I turned fourteen.

That year, I volunteered to be a candy striper at the local hospital. Excited at the opportunity to start in my chosen nursing field, I purchased the red-and-white-striped uniform and dyed a pair of shoes white, as required. I didn't know what to expect since I had never been in a hospital before—at least not since my birth. The first day as a candy striper, I worked at the front desk.

On the bulletin board behind the reception desk, I alphabetized room assignments to match the person's name, and I delivered fragrant flowers to the patients. I loaded the cheerful bouquets on the steel portable cart and walked the beige, sterile hallways, delivering each one to its respective recipient. I gave a floral arrangement to an old man with numerous wires and tubes connected to him. He looked so sick. He didn't or couldn't acknowledge me. I went from room to room delivering the flowers.

With each passing room, I thought, "These people are so sick; it's depressing."

After that day, I wondered, "How could I ever work in a hospital? Look at all these sick people."

I didn't know how I could handle it. I didn't like the intense feelings and their overpowering sensations. Of course they were intense; I had already shifted into suppressing my emotions. I had begun morphing from Beth to Liz. Beth wanted to be a nurse, not Liz.

I had various assignments at the hospital, but the one I liked best was in the administration office. What might have been the most boring job for others was something I found rewarding. I alphabetized papers and put them in file folders. That was so simple. I realized I could work in an office.

While the candy striper disappointment dashed my childhood aspiration to become a nurse, I quickly leveraged the experience to create a new plan for an office job. I knew Mom had been a secretary for many years before her current scriptwriter and story-editor position at the movie studio. I could follow her example as an office worker.

Mom had always encouraged our artistic development, and acting was one of her many forms of expression. She included us in as many dramatic performances as she could. There were times when the entire family performed in theater roles, such as a play about a pioneer woman trekking the plains with her splendid wedding slippers stowed away.

We also appeared as extras or in bit parts at the movie studio where she worked. While I was growing up, Mom acted more than she painted or sketched, but they were all hobbies. Mom often told us that her artistic talent had been fostered, even when it wasn't as good as she thought it was. She apparently became increasingly better, since a children's magazine published some of her illustrations.

At some point after fourth grade, I concluded that artistry or creativity was not part of my inheritance or capability. However, as a businesswoman, I could prove I was as good as my talented mother who had unwittingly set the bar so high. She did not place the bar for me; I set it myself.

I reasoned that learning secretarial skills would be helpful, and something I could use to provide additional support for my future family, if needed. Then, when the children of my imagined future were in school, I could work part time and be home to greet them. Of course, before they were school age, I would be a stay-at-home mother, since I didn't want to repeat Mom's working-mother scenario. I still thought about other part-time career possibilities.

When we were discussing our futures, my friend Meg said she was planning to marry immediately after high school graduation, even though that was a few years away and she had no boyfriend. Until then, I had never considered that I shouldn't go to a university. It seemed so automatic. All of my sisters had attended college. What Meg said didn't sway me. I wanted to enroll in a university, and I was also determined to earn an academic scholarship.

I floundered around in my later teen years, uncertain what to declare as a major since there's no such thing as a bachelor's degree in secretarial skills. I wanted to discover what I was excited about, so I tried a logical approach.

In my second year of college, I went to a career-guidance class to sort through the possibilities and identify what most interested me. The career assessments pointed to two appealing options: social worker and speech pathologist.

As part of the class, I interviewed people currently doing social work and speech pathology. The social worker seemed inundated with others' problems, and I ruled it out as psychologically taxing.

The speech pathologist was inspiring. She worked with aphasic patients—those who had lost their ability to communicate. I had already taken a fascinating linguistics class. The speech pathologist combined the whole "helping people" theme with language, so it was irresistible. Relieved that I had finally found a worthwhile replacement for nursing, I declared it as my major.

However, I didn't end up pursuing that degree because Gillis and I married shortly afterward. I took a hiatus from school and waited for our financial situation to improve. When we were newlyweds, he explained that I needed to find a more suitable degree that I could use when we would move to Nigeria in an estimated ten years. I understood his logic, and reluctantly agreed, but still I was disheartened. I had taken years to solve my career dilemma, but it no longer seemed a viable choice.

Several months later, my boss, Marilyn, asked me to expand beyond my secretarial duties and take over the office manager and personnel functions. At first, I refused. I didn't think I could do it. Marilyn knew better and cleverly asked me to combine memos written over the years into an employee handbook. A few special projects later, I was carrying out the role I had not been confident enough to accept formally…and enjoying it. When I resumed studies via night school the following year, I figured I should major in what I was already doing—human resources.

80C3

When I reflected on this whole sequence of events related to my human resources career and passion, it reminded me of the song "Do You Love Me," in the play and movie, *Fiddler on the Roof.* Tevye asks his wife Golde, for the first time in twenty-five years, if she loves him. They realize, from the inception of an arranged marriage, they grew to love each other but never explicitly acknowledged the love.

I used to both admire and envy people who are passionate about what they do. I did not recognize this emotion in myself. I suppressed the sensation.

I didn't find my human resources career. It found me. Although not a nurse, through human resources I achieved my childhood desire to help people—all the time. I helped them in ways different from nursing, using intangible skills playing to my strengths. Like an arranged marriage, after twenty-eight years, it was gratifying to know: I had been passionate about what I did.

Evaluating this, I thought, "Of course, I wouldn't have recognized this before, because I couldn't. When feelings were suppressed, how could I acknowledge passion?"

I also discovered through reconnecting with my anger that the key reason I didn't feel or recognize passion is due to the duality of its connection with anger. They are two parts of an extreme. When I didn't allow myself to feel fury, I couldn't sense its polar opposite—passion.

With my discovery that I actually loved what I did in my human resources career, it led me to ponder a deeper question. What exactly did I love most about it? Could I extract the most precious professional gem and use it to obliterate my insatiable emptiness?

I knew there was a more magnificent, exquisite jewel within me. I resolved to unearth it.

Questions

Questions in my mind
Unceasing
Answers yet to find
Increasing
Trust in what I know
Faltering
Constraints do erode
Unlimiting

6
POETIC PARTURITION

A new outlet for all the emotions I had been submerging...

❧ 2013 ☙

Still looking for some way to love myself, I decided to use some frequent-flyer miles and visit my dear friend, Layla, who lived in Europe. Layla was also going through a hard time, and I felt if we spent some time together connecting, it would be therapeutic for us both. We decided to spend the upcoming holiday on a girls' weekend in Paris, not far from where she was living.

I made the decision and told Gillis. He would have wanted me to consult him first. He didn't want to spend the holiday alone. I didn't want to ask his opinion. I knew I would chicken out if I did. I decided that no matter what, I was going to visit Layla. Somehow, deep within me, I knew I needed this experience. I didn't want to have a heated argument. I wondered how I could express my need without making it more hurtful than it already was to Gillis.

In the shower, thoughts seeped in. The words of an original poem poured into place. Do you like the metaphor? My soul cleansed itself of the past interaction. In the cascading water, an idea sprang forth. Right, I wrote a poem. Gillis was traveling in another city at the time, so I sent it to him.

Alone I Stay

Alone I stay.
He goes away.
"Just for a few";
That's rarely true

A tropical prison.
Want to have fun.
No beach today;
He's gone away.

Don't alone drive.
Crazies here thrive.
Careful where you walk;
Future kidnappers stalk.

No family near,
Or anyone dear.
Need some girl time,
Get away from the clime.

"Be true to me,
Lack meaning, you see."
Honey says, "No.
Forbid you to go."

Totally pissed,
If I persist.
Cancel my plan?
Stay with my man?

He'll come back,
But won't unpack.
Soon, one day,
He'll go anyway.

"Just for a few";
That's rarely true.
Alone I stay,
Screwed either way.

Gillis responded with his own *poem*. "Fantastic," I thought. That was already a shift, though he still was not thrilled with the idea of my trip. I wrote him another poem in response.

Girl Time

I am full of melancholy
You think it's folly

I know you don't understand
Why I'd stick with this plan

Just a few days
To help my mental craze

Indulge girl time si'l vous plaît
From us, it doesn't take away

You're still my main squeeze
Come to Lagos the sixteenth, please

I was pleased that I expressed myself in an authentic and heartfelt way, even though there was irritation underlying it. Indeed, this was a shift in our communication.

Still not enthralled with the idea that I would spend the holiday with Layla instead of him, Gillis wished me a pleasant trip.

ᘓᘐ

Layla has a beautiful, beaming smile that reminds me of Julia Roberts, and a ready, infectious laugh. Her chestnut hair cascades loosely to her waist, a little longer than mine. We drive several hours by car. In our mutual misery, my tears are contagious. We talk about all our plans and fears while the wooded countryside gives way to bustling cities. We stop in Brussels for lunch. My ears perk up, trying to discern the different languages that both customers and polyglot servers are speaking.

The square we walk through is surrounded by magnificent buildings, hundreds of years old. Each building's wall serves as a common one with the next. Some ways to distinguish among the buildings are colors, styles, decorative façades, and roofs. The architecture is breathtaking. Domes, golden spires, and beautiful statues ornately adorn and crown each building. Then, as we enter the French countryside, vineyards and farm cottages dot picturesque, green rolling hills.

It is my first time in Paris, but Layla has been here before. We trek the numerous flights of stairs to the Eiffel Tower observation deck. What a splendid panorama of the skyline, old and new neighborhoods, and the major landmarks. It is similar to what I remember seeing in movies, and it feels familiar.

When we arrive at the Cathedral of Notre Dame, a nearby building is undergoing renovation. A huge painted canvas drapes across the building, creating an appealing façade. We can't see all the work going on below. I think, "They still manage to make it look nice even when there's messy and ugly construction beneath." I ponder, "Maybe there is a parallel with me."

We walk to the cathedral's other side, where it isn't crowded with visitors jostling to enter. I spend time noting all the sculptures carved in the rock and placed atop the spires plus the numerous gargoyles leering with their freaky faces. I am fascinated by the painstaking detail in the statues, artwork, and ornamentation.

The bridges, architecture, and sense of history are characteristics I have always liked about Europe. The preserved, centuries-old buildings exude majesty.

I have an incredible connection time with Layla. We talk at length about our feelings of failure and our concerns. We've known each other since before we were mothers. We share the passion about motherhood. It's been ingrained for so long. We are both supportive but not trying obsessively to solve each other's depressive problems. I expose my heartache—and Beth, the part of me she never quite met before, connects with her, too.

While the emotional connection with Layla is crucial on this trip, equally important is the creative stimulation. The ambiance serves as a reminder of the majesty we create when we allow our inspiration to flourish. I'm excited by my new poetic handiwork, and more and more poems pour from my fingertips to the page.

Mourning

Threats three decades long,
Ring familiar,
Ring painful,
Ring unchanged.
I will mourn the loss.

Dreams of another,
Seem like mine.
They are noble.
They are driven.
They are longstanding.

What dreams are my creations?
I had only one.
I lost the hope.
I no longer know.
I mourn the loss.

To seek a new dream,
To replace the one,
To regain hope,
By searching will I know.
I will mourn the less.

I had a cleansing journey. My epiphany in the shower, when the poetry poured, was more than a metaphor. As I lathered my body, it washed a wave of creativity through my soul and purged messy communication patterns of the past. The Paris trip also formed a rising surge of empowerment. It helped me do something for only myself. It was liberating. At times, I felt peace and enjoyment.

I was shocked and excited that I had expressed myself creatively and poetically. Most significantly, my previously unknown creativity and a different angle on an unrecognized passion were beginning to emerge.

I remembered I wrote a few poems when I was in junior high or high school. "Were they any good?" I wondered. I dug out papers from my filing-cabinet collection. Those poems were sad. "Hmm, was I sad then, too?" I pondered. I had already realized depression had followed me for a long time, though I hadn't labeled it that way.

Had I been interested in poetry and not acknowledged that, either? I had won awards in high school for memorizing and reciting poetry in the district's German-language contests. Maybe there was a long-standing connection.

I recalled a fifth-grade assignment where each student had created a short filmstrip and video. I chose several passages from the collection, *Don't You Turn Back: Poems by Langston Hughes* (Alfred A. Knopf, 1969). I illustrated and narrated several of his poems. I extracted haunting selections such as "Ennui" and "Suicide's Note." This couldn't be typical for a ten year old. It seemed connected to some darkness already sitting unacknowledged and waiting. Looking back, I could see the gloom would build over the next forty years until it no longer lay submerged in the dam of emotions near the Beth cave. It would burst at the moment when I would release all hope, in spasmodic paralysis, on my kitchen floor.

The Artist's Way encouraged me to look at free associations by completing its initial prompts. I wrote unfiltered, first-impulse responses regarding my conditioned beliefs about artists and creativity.

> *Excerpt Seven*
> *My parents think*…artists are talented and can use their talents in a hobby—but will probably never support a family.
> *What makes me feel weird about this recovery*…is that I'm not an artist. I just want to feel like I'm more creative or have a creative outlet that isn't just business. I also want to figure out if I dropped all this creative stuff I'd done as a child because I wasn't interested, wasn't good, or whatever the issue is/was.
> *Learning to trust myself is*…probably harder when it comes to this type of thing where there's no proof of talent or capability, and I don't feel like I measure up to other family members' gifts.
> *If it didn't sound so crazy, I'd*…write.

From the depths of my depression, an exquisite gift was emerging—creativity. Poetry was a new outlet for all the emotions I had been submerging. It was a double present. It allowed me to both express and release long-suppressed artistry and emotion. When I felt extreme emotion—happy, frustrated, sad, or depressed—words flowed. This was new to me because I never considered myself as imaginative. I wrote the "Inspiration" poem about that. Irony. I have a super-talented family. As child six of six, I didn't think, by the time I came along, anything was left over.

Inspiration

"Creativeness skipped me,"
that's what I told myself.
Mother was an artist, writer,
thespian—awards on the shelf.

A pair of ceramic slippers,
icon of a most beloved play,
hung on the childhood wall
reminding each and every day.

Decided no point in trying
I simply couldn't compete
my amateurish attempts
were woefully un-replete.

Don't get me wrong,
I dabbled, in films and plays
as well, from the age of five,
and kept their gesturing ways.

Maybe I wasn't good enough,
or could be I didn't dare,
once I had grown and acting
became a past family affair.

Took one art class in school,
penned egg, square, and sphere;
labored on their shadowing,
alas artistry was nowhere near.

Convinced talent in my genes
Mother Nature had omitted.
Had no understanding then,
practice perfects the committed.

So focused on the logical,
my left brain into gear;
threw self into business,
three decades and a year.

Suddenly found myself
in a most unusual place.
Seemed to come from nowhere,
rhyming phrases filled my space.

Now in the course of common,
notice my own thoughts,
and write them down a-plenty
in many differing jots.

Perhaps a gift was always
mine unopened to discover.
Words newborn and given life
inspired by dear Mother.

My paradigm began to change.

Excerpt Eight
    I feel fortunate to have waded through the dregs of depression, and seeing this even more developed sense of self emerging...I am creative in ways that sometimes surprise me.

I acknowledged one passion in human resources that I had not known existed. The dawning idea of poetry becoming another aspiration intrigued me. Even with this new awareness, I was still missing a connection to acknowledge and unleash my complete creativity. I also had to unlock a hidden, closeted passion.

We return to my dark thoughts, introduce my intense critical self-talk, then move to when I first began questioning my passion and meaning in earnest.

VACATING THE VOID

The one thing that gives my life

meaning seems unobtainable...

7
CHAWING CHATTER

I call it the propagandizer...

When I wrote this poem describing the evening I decided to kill myself, it had been more than a year since the event. Looking back, I still know the feeling. I can touch the emotions, but they do not immobilize and hold me hostage. If your inner voice screams obscenities at you right now, feel free to skip to the next chapter and come back at any time to my malevolent mind.

Whirlpool

My body falls limp, heaped
onto the cool stained concrete floor.
Agony of decades escapes,
unfettered from my deepest recess,
and with my banshee-like scream,
I exhale all hope.

The trigger is not the issue.
The familial patterns familiar,
but after so many times,

and who knows what contributory else,
I am emotionally exhausted
and lie in sobbing, spasmodic paralysis.

Eyes open but not seeing,
the whirlpool of my thoughts
blinding the physical.
Only the mental remains,
sucking me deep, down
into a spiral abyss of fear,
loathing, and hopelessness.

There's no point anymore.
The one thing that gives me meaning
I fear in that instant will never be
in the way I long for and mentally paint.

No more struggle needed;
I am superfluous and ineffective.
I give up. Now to choose how.

No instant means at my disposal;
I search for ideas.
The perfect site seems to appear.
I read of another's attempts and failures,
and then words of caution and statistics
about methods and their accompanying success rates
as well as unintended consequences,
when attempts don't go as planned
and they live in misery, disfigured and worse.

It feeds my intellectual famine.
The mental anguish is bad enough.
I don't want physical torture, too.
Going to sleep forever sounds nice,

but not having my stomach pumped,
or neurological problems to persist
if for some reason I continue to stay.
And I don't have those kinds of pills, anyway.

My death quest is disrupted in the midst of research.
Confronted with love and admonition,
I'm unable to latch onto the invisible ladder
and still can't climb from the depth
of that mental whirlpool,
still sucking out all hope
and desire for a future.

But the website is still open,
and I'm no longer reading.

Sleep rescues without medication—
a temporary respite, just for the night,
not one forever as I had imagined.
Still distraught and fairly listless,
I roll out of the comfort of my bed,
and see a glimpse of hope
unfold in the morning scene before me.

It's just the littlest ray,
but still there sparkling faintly before me.
I blink the weeping water
before wiping away.
An inkling of relief to brighten my dull soul.

Though the whirlpool still churns inside,
inviting me for a spin and
at the slightest provocation,
I willingly dive in.

Family's quick to notice now
that distant look in my glazed eyes—
when I've disconnected from their presence
and mentally dance in circles,
downwardly descending into despair.
They quickly toss me verbal safety nets,
reeling me back to them.

Always the strong one,
but not anymore.
Feel so weak and empty,
no longer replete.

Sharing with my sisters
of the soul and of the body,
just how drained I feel.
Discover I am not the only one.

Surprising solace when
our deepest distress revealed.
Some have learned techniques
to fend off the demons
before they fully emerge.
Others are still in the midst
of the battle, fending off
their own fiendish selves as foes.

Sharing stories is cathartic.
Causes of the pain differ,
though the emotions are the same—
shame, fear, regret, hopelessness.
Things not within our control
happening to those we cherish.
Feeling we should have or should do more
when we've done all we knew.

We are all connected
in this one and precious life.
No matter how trivial or overwhelming
someone else's provocation seems,
it is always in the eye of the beholder,
a tsunami capable of instant flooding
with the same surge of devastating emotions.

Seeing the goodness in them,
realizing they see it in me too,
helps to recover a sense of self.
We are so much the same.
Slowly judging self—less harshly.
Forgiving self as much as others.
Finding meaning and purpose
in new and different ways.

Knowing that the whirlpool
will beckon now and always.
Recognizing emotional weather patterns
and learning to steer clear.
Building a repertoire of self-care.
Meeting one's own needs is not selfish;
it's the only way to ensure
we can continue to serve others,
bringing joy to self and our treasured ones,
with the love and caring we all deserve.

The whirlpool beckoned most when I tried the hardest to ignore my inner critic. I call it the propagandizer. It echoed loudest in my thoughts when I was feeling hopeless, empty, and depressed. Suppressing it didn't help. I needed to acknowledge it but didn't have the tools to allow me to process through it. I describe how I feel about my propagandizer, and its critical chatter, in the following poem.

Propagandizer

Incessant chattering,
Watching every move.
Waiting to pounce and
Pronounce my foibles,
Vile critic within.

Looming shapeless, faceless,
Creeping ever menacingly near.
Claws like razors on my back,
Vicious attack of everything
Critic screams I lack.

I must say when in despair,
Critic swims gleefully everywhere:
Backstroking in failure,
Dog paddling in worthlessness,
Butterflying in fear.

"Shut up," I say in anguish,
But critic has only a
Merciless mouth; no ears.

8
FLIPPING FAILURE FOCUS

Yesterday's failures surmounted

are today's successes...

Hues

funky depressing
blue

cloudy storming
grey

alternate exploding
red

calmness returning
yellow

naturally appreciating
green

cheerfully soaking
orange

enveloped healing
white

๕ 2012 ෬

Before I discovered my emerging creativity or acknowledged my professional passion, I had a void. It was more than career or inspiration. This was about family. What else in my life would give me meaning besides my family?

Excerpt Nine

Very depressed last night; seems to hit me evenings the worst. Thinking about sleeping pills and just going to sleep forever. Contemplating the meaning of life. When the meaning of life is whatever you decide it is, and you can't decide, or nothing feels compelling enough, then what is life?

I used to believe I *knew* all these answers because religion taught them to me. But thinking for myself now, and looking at all or many possibilities, that answer, that question, presents no clear answer.

They are whatever people believe them to be. So there I am, thinking, "Really, what's the point?" I am so out of whack with myself, and I can't control whatever happens in my family. At the same time, all I can think of is *failure*—even though logically it's not all up to me.

The one thing that gives my life meaning seems unobtainable.

I lacked meaning. When did I have meaning? I thought I had it. Having "perfect family" moments gave me meaning. It was what I latched onto. When my propagandizer taunted me that my family would never be the way I had imagined, the whirlpool of despair sucked me in.

If I couldn't have this fantasized family that I'd spent nearly three decades shaping, then I had failed. It was never going to happen. It was then I pursued the questions, "What else do I want?" and "What would give meaning to *me*, independent of others?"

I looked at what the research showed. I read what others felt. I had to shift a longstanding paradigm I had clung to ever since I can remember. It was not easy. I didn't know how to uncover it. I asked myself questions the books I read told me to answer. They were not satisfying. They didn't fill the emptiness, the nothingness.

I reflected a lot and had some vague ideas. I also knew some of my illusions, especially around my idealized family, I had to release. They were driving me to anguish.

I contemplated, "How could I discover for myself what gave me meaning? What reason did I wish to continue living? What was the point of it all?"

I was still struggling to find what was meaningful for me.

Family and career consumed my whole identity—my personal family and my work family. All of it was a family thing for me. It was not the family itself, but me. What I wanted out of it was to complete the hole in my whole, the gnawing emptiness I had within myself, expecting that relationships with others would fill it.

The work I did was okay, but I was often so depressed that it didn't give me the satisfaction I'd had in the past. I beat myself up mentally about what I *should* be doing that I simply didn't have the energy to *do*. I was emotionally and physically exhausted most of the time. There would be periods where it would seem okay, but any little spark would set me off. I would ruminate instead of reflect. I was not learning lessons from the past. My chawing propagandizer judged and proclaimed myself inadequate in oh, so many ways.

When I was looking for meaning and purpose, asking myself, "What do I really want?" I could not answer. I desperately thought I wanted the answers and would yearn for clarity. In reality, I covertly didn't want clarity.

Do you know why? If I had clarity, if I knew what I wanted, that means I would need to *do* something about it. Without clarity, I don't need to take action. I can continue living the veiled lies I tell myself, remaining a victim in my own dysfunctional drama.

Comfortable Discomfort

When you try to help me,
And I dismiss each suggestion,
Proclaiming none of them will work,
It's not personal at all.

I am comfortable in my discomfort,
And I'll stay awhile more.

In my self-imposed perspective,
Where martyr to my maladies,
I know somehow the answer
Within me deeply lies, yet I deny.

I am comfortable in my discomfort,
And I'll stay awhile more.

You may wish for clarity, but be blocked as I was. I created a mirage where I thought asking the question was enough. I was deceiving myself. I paralyzed myself with fearful thoughts of a future that never materialized.

I didn't want to take action because I was afraid of the outcome. I feared I would fail, and that meant I was a failure. Certainly, everyone has some fear of failure. However, not everyone wraps his or her entire worth in failure. To begin confronting this, I chose to explore what failure meant to me.

I realized yesterday's failures surmounted are today's successes. We learn through our failures. Others love to hear how we overcame challenges—those initial failures—that we eventually shifted into success.

I suppose I would have found it impossible to publicly share my failure, my depression, my inability to keep myself happy and self-loving while I was mired in that state. Although I discovered later that the deep depression I had was actually a gift, a catalyst, it certainly didn't feel that way at the time.

Outcome Dependent

Shadowy fears realized;
Desires, wants, expectations unmet.

Finance, relationship, career—
Players and situations change,
Taunting, haunting,
Theme remains.
Tightening breast,
Tearing eye,
Rumination.

I am a failure.
I am a failure.
I am a failure.

Critical analysis
Intellectualizes,
Objective mind mapping,
Exploring data points.
Overreaction,
Disaggregation,
Reflection.

Am I a failure?
Am I a failure?

Am I a failure?

Successes in some,
Just not this one,
That I cling to wanting
A different outcome.
Specific result,
Not defining
Me individually.

It is a failure.
It is a failure.
It is a failure.

Peeking paradigm perspective,
Balancing polarized scale,
Positives outweigh negatives,
In the life sum total.
Learning,
Growing,
Opportunities.

I am not a failure.
I am not a failure.
I am not a failure.

Flip the failure focus
As the motivator, instead.
Shift to see success,
Lining silver-edged cloud.
In duality, light and shadow,
Rain and shine, blend for growth.

I pondered my issues surrounding failure for many months. One day, a word popped into my head about my association with failure: unlovable.

I was talking to Kristine about my newfound insight that failure equaled unlovable. As I described my word correlation, I found myself telling Kristine it meant, "If I did not succeed, Mom and Dad wouldn't love me."

That surprised me to hear the words out loud. It hadn't been a conscious thought before. I puzzled this statement audibly. I realized tears were welling in my eyes, and my throat was constricting as I said those words.

Clearly, there was a deep emotion attached to it—a somatic connection with the emotion I hadn't recognized. I mulled aloud to Kristine that it didn't make sense to me. It wasn't logical. After all, our parents had both been dead for a decade. I didn't need their approval today. I also knew they loved me.

I also wondered, "Could it be linked to the transformation from Beth to Liz?" There was something deeper there. I believed someday that unconscious part of me would connect with the conscious. For then, it was enough to have the awareness that the physical reaction and emotion around failure ensnared my self-worth. Acknowledging its existence, examining a fear, and shifting it from the shadows, weakened its power.

Repose

My lidded visions
Speak to me
In colors
Purple, gold, and white

Focus my breath
Inhale deeply
To the innermost
Fill to capacity

Hold
Count
One
Two
Three

Release
Slowly
Exhale
One
Two
Three

Repeat
Repeat

My troubles dance
In front of me

Bathed transparent in
This healing
Light

Not quite the
Same

Softening their edges
And my
Plight

I feel you
Fully

Anger
Anxiety
Fear

Nested in my
Bosom
Gut
Mind

I see you
All
Clinging
There

I ignore you no more

Each serves a purpose
Yet, just now
It's time
To shelter in rest
Leave the room
Close the door

I'll wake you
When you're needed from
Sweet repose
To urge me
Into action

Excuse me
While
I bask in
The rising rays
Of surrender and
Contentment

9
PARASITIC PROBLEM

I had no lifeblood to suck and was famished...

I vacillated. I concluded that my void was about meaning. Then I would doubt myself. Was it really about meaning? Perhaps it was purely the empty-nester syndrome setting in harder with me. My capable children did not need the interventions I could offer anymore. They had grown into wonderful adults with their own ideas about how to live their lives. I didn't agree with all their decisions. I tried not to force my perspective. Yet, simultaneously I obsessed, trying to fix what I considered their problems.

I remember late one night, sitting and writing in my small, black-leather notebook about how painful the lack of meaning felt. What was the point? What good was I? My propagandizer shrieked that I had done a terrible job as a mother. Now grown, my kids didn't need me.

Empty Nest

Empty is the nest.
Pushed them out.
Time to grow.
Wings to spread.

Soar so high,
On your own.
No wonder why,
Feeling empty like a nest.

I realized I had become so embroiled in helping other people—especially Gillis and my kids—with their dreams and goals, I had to ask myself some questions about what it was I most wanted for myself. Besides human resources, did I have anything uniquely mine to pursue?

I recalled in my late twenties, I once went to a counselor who described my entanglement with a role-play. She took a cushion from the couch.

She said, "This pillow represents a problem. I am carrying a problem. I complain how burdensome the issue is. You see it and begin to help me hold the pillow—the problem."

Then I took the other half of the pillow and began to carry it with the counselor.

The counselor continued, "Eventually, the other person may stop holding their side of the pillow. What happens then?"

She dropped her hands, and I was carrying it by myself.

I said, "I'm holding the pillow alone. I realize that after some time, I'm the only one carrying it—and then I want to *throw* it back."

That was a decades-old conversation. It began to dawn on me that this pillow analogy *happens all the time* in smaller and larger ways.

I also began to comprehend that it's not the other person's fault. I always offered, but I didn't know when to stop, how to help in a healthy way, or how to express my needs. I was the frustrated one. I was the one who needed to change.

Say What Needs to be Said

Playing in my head
Rehearsing just the right tempo, emphasis, meter
A script you never hear

Would you understand?

I am a thespian with long, intricate soliloquies
With an audience
Entirely of me, myself, and I

Would you even try?

Showed you the dialog of scene one
After a page, you were done.

Say what needs to be said

So very good am I
At doing that with colleagues
There, mind matters more than heart
Though I give them both
I can always replace a job
A lover? A child? Well, that's different

Say what needs to be said

Improvisation was never my forte
When I'm not another character
No other mask for me to hide behind
Speaking from the heart and soul
Would I even find the words aloud to

Say what needs to be said?

I had goals and dreams I had been discussing and working toward with Gillis. Were any of them *my* goals and dreams? I wanted to be supportive, but I enmeshed my support. I had trouble with boundaries. I had taken responsibility for the meaning, passion, and purpose that Gillis, Victoria, Kenneth, and Christopher were pursuing. I had adopted them as mine. I was so busy helping them pursue their interests that I was living a life of meaning vicariously. I was like a parasite feeding on their problems, meaning, and passions. When their dreams and goals changed direction, it created a mismatch in my trajectory. Wrenched from my host, I had no lifeblood to suck and was famished.

I didn't know what my own meaning was. I didn't know because I couldn't feel it. I hadn't practiced it myself in the way I could understand it. I had overused my helper skill so much that it had become negative for me—like being a high achiever who becomes a workaholic. To the extreme, it is harmful. When in balance, it is beneficial. I was out of whack—and I had been out of balance so long that I didn't know what equilibrium looked or felt like.

Instead of urging others to take their pillow back, or not taking their pillow in the first place, I would throw their pillow at them, metaphorically speaking. I would think that by throwing it back, I had solved the problem. Then another pillow emerged. The cycle started again. These were definite repetitions.

You will notice in your own life as you evaluate and observe issues, they are not isolated; they are all connected.

Eventually, I concluded the first, most important, relationship is with myself. Blending my shunned Beth self to explore my full self would be the only way to achieve peace. I am the only person who can ever fill my void. Only I can brighten the darkness with light or douse the light with darkness. I remembered Edgar Guest's poem, *Myself*, that I'd memorized in sixth grade. It inspired my own version.

Love Myself

I want to love myself, and so,
I want to greater myself know.

I don't want to feel, with the setting sun,
Full of loathing for what I've done.

Put away the guilt and shame.
Cast away self and other blame.

The future's uncertain and can be
Fearfully sucking away energy.

It's been exhausting trying to cope.
Time to reclaim my faltering hope.

Shift my thinking, shift my life.
I don't need this turbulent strife.

Life's a lesson for me to learn.
Help me uncover for what I yearn.

Live not just for others, but for myself.
Time for healing and emotional health.

Envision dreams and my power,
I vow to live life fully in this hour.

Saying I needed to love myself was easy. Doing it wasn't. I knew I needed to feel better about myself to fill the void, but I often filled it with distractions and activities like surfing the internet and watching TV. Once the activities stopped, the emptiness came back.

In the deepest parts of my depression, you would not have noticed my aching emptiness and despair if you were not in my inner circle. I went to work. I joked, and I laughed. I *performed.* I wore the mask of Liz well. It was comfortable.

You did not see me in my alone times. You did not see the nights I came home and vegetated in front of the television. I knew I was vegetating. I knew it was a distraction. I would weep at some of the stories. They would dig up despondency, and help me to feel more alone in my city of over 18 million while Gillis traveled and Victoria, Kenneth, and Christopher lived their lives thousands of miles away in the US.

TV

pixelation immersion absorption
distortion dereliction
distraction
numbing
desensitizing hammering
pestering paralyzing ruminating

I placed phone calls and wrote letters. Social media helped me to keep track of all the masks everybody else was wearing in my extended circle and all their busyness.

That sounds cynical. I mean merely that we often put our best foot forward on social media, showing images of our happy family, all smiling. Every family has disagreements and areas of intense heartache. We don't show those to everyone. Some of us don't even acknowledge it. I get it. I lived it.

My Cup Runneth

I fill myself up with
distractions:
television, internet, idle talk.

None of it matters.
It's like junk food—
it fills but does not nourish—
unsatisfying.

My cup runneth empty.

I go to a party.
Mingle and mix.
Talk about things
no one really cares about.
Distractions:
feel exciting in the moment.
When the people are gone,

My cup runneth empty.

Only me, alone.
My thoughts
backward, forward,
in time in my mind.
Distractions:
not in the present.

My cup runneth empty.

Empty gnawing.
No accomplishment matters,
large or small—
only what's next,
pushing me forward.

My cup runneth empty.

I fill myself up with
plans for the future.
Hope to feel better,
or is that to fill better?

My cup runneth empty.

It isn't half full.
It isn't half empty.
It isn't the wrong size.
It simply evaporates
with the distractions.

What seemed so filling,
unachievable now, is unfulfilling.
Leaves me with feelings;

My cup runneth empty.

Recognizing I had lived vicariously, I continued looking for
my own meaning, solutions to reduce the vast void, and ways to
blend myself. To bring together Beth and Liz, I needed to
resurface the teenage trauma that fragmented me.

SHADOWED SELF

I met my shadow...

She was me, and I love her now...

10
BETH'S BETRAYAL

I didn't want to associate with Beth...

ᖇ 1974 ᘓ

We are alone in the large expanse of the home. Standing at five feet eight inches, I have only about an inch to add before I stop growing and reach my full height. My brown hair has lost its honey-colored highlights from childhood and thickly cascades straight along my back, touching my waistline. The sun-kissed speckles dotting my nose and face are fading into a smoother complexion as I mature into adolescence. I'm wearing my baby-blue turtleneck body suit and flower-sprinkled red skirt. The turtleneck's weave gives the illusion of vertical ribboning. The body suit is like a leotard but has snaps at the crotch. I push the long sleeves to three-quarters length, ending a little below my elbows, and revealing my lightly freckled forearms.

We are now in the master bedroom. I see myself from a different vantage point, as if in a dream or a movie. I am not in my body.

Even as tall as she is, his intimidating physique and stature still tower over the young girl with long, brown hair and fading freckles. With strength and determination, he traps her. He pins her down. That girl is lying on the bottom edge of the golden, crushed velvet bedspread. He pushes the flower-sprinkled red skirt aside, exposing her bare thighs. Only her baby-blue body suit remains. She pleads for this to go no further. She is terrified.

I am terrified.

He urges me to undress as he has done. He hovers over me in his indigo-blue bikini briefs. I am crying and pleading. I fear the threat of physical violation. Somehow, he stops before complete disrobing and actual penetration. I am grateful for the extra level of protection my baby-blue body suit and its snaps provide. My underwear is intact.

My virginity is preserved, but he has utterly betrayed my trust.

 ∞ 

I was thirteen. I had no intention of sex. I had not expressed any desire with this young man and had no idea how it led to this. We had no precursors. We had no natural intimacy escalation. We had been completely platonic. We were relatives, after all.

I remember how I felt during the encounter: the terror—and after—the shame. I felt so responsible. I must have done something I couldn't understand to encourage this surprise attack. I felt so dirty, and the unworthiness played in my mind. To tell someone about this would reveal a secret, filthy shame. I told no one then and stashed the secret. I was only relieved it had gone no further than it had.

The damage, however, was the final nail in my coffin of victimization. I wanted to bury that feeling. I didn't like the sensation. It was then I unwittingly became a Vulcan.

It was not a conscious decision. It was a conclusion driven by the understanding that emotions equated to vulnerability, a victim. I did not want to feel like a victim. I wanted to feel powerful. Beth was emotional, and that meant she was vulnerable. Beth was a victim. I didn't want to associate with

Beth. I wanted to forever bury Beth along with the feelings and the victimization.

It took me a few years to admit to anyone what had happened that afternoon on the golden, crushed velvet bedspread. Finally, I admitted it to Mom. My betrayer had asked for forgiveness, and I had already given it. He was not much older than I was, and I could rationalize it in the impetuousness of his youth.

I did not forgive myself, however, for whatever I perceived may have been my unintentional role in enticing such a situation. There was still shame, guilt, and dirtiness around it. However, by then, I had already stepped into my newfound persona and become Liz. The transformation was complete. I was not ready to visit that weak victim, Beth, anymore. Let her stay buried in her cave forever.

I had an emerging sense that the pain of keeping Beth hidden away was greater than the distress I would face by integrating her. Facing this trauma began the process of reconnecting with emotion and Beth. I started with a reflection on my teenage years.

From The Shadows

Wispy specter sucking savory radiance
Into your opaque, oppressive cave,
I ignore you,
And pretend you go away.

My negative thoughts, beliefs,
I choose not to feel,
Are your feast.
You become strong.

Outside rays rare burn bright.
They bend, drawn magnetically to you.
What passion I have

Feels pragmatically hollow.

Trifecta of fear, guilt, and shame
Pushes my spirit aside to your side.
I languish.
I become weak.

You are not a comforting companion.
I seek purposeful meaning.
You offer nothing.
I see momentary glimpses
Of luminosity before you suck them
Of their soulfulness.

The chasm below is dark.
I walk warily toward the black hole.
You challenge my path.
I battle you victorious,
Rip away your hideous mask
To reveal my face.

Untwisting with self-love,
Compassion, and acceptance
As we blend in light and shadow,
My deeds both dark and bright,
No longer dual to duel,
Joined solely in soul.
Rebirthing has begun.

11
DANCING WITH DARKNESS

Sometimes you need to kill the good

to make way for the great...

ℬ 2014 ℭ

While examining my teenage years, I saw that I was already artfully subduing my emotions by the age of fourteen. I recalled watching *The Other Side of the Mountain*. It was a movie about a professional skier, Jill Kinmont, who lost the use of her legs.

The theater lights brightened, and we sat in our seats waiting to leave. My friend, Meg, feeling moved by the compelling biography, turned to look at me. I saw the thin, black streaks of mascara trailing beneath her glistening brown eyes. She expressed surprise that my own blue-green eyes were dry.

I joked and told Meg, "I was all cried out in my childhood."

Meg proclaimed, "Wow, you have a heart of ice."

Meg's judgment made me feel bad. I tucked away her jab, but that didn't bring any tears, either. It was an emotion to look at curiously before tossing it behind Beth's dam, where I stowed all the other emotions I didn't want to deal with.

Queen of Ice

Spreads the frozen layer
thickly over troubled,
churning waters.
You'd never know
the nether
anxiety and fear.

She doesn't think these
one day will melt ice,
causing gaping fluid wounds
she won't know
how to heal with
frosty suppression.

Beth was a total empath. She didn't merely feel her own feelings. She felt everyone else's too. Remember the emotional intelligence assessment? My access to anger was almost nonexistent, but my "empathy-compassion dimension" for other people was extraordinary—and accurate. That compassion didn't extend to me.

My own anguish was enough. Through Beth, I didn't want to feel everyone else's. That's engulfing, especially when I couldn't enforce appropriate boundaries around those emotions. It seemed easier to shun.

While Beth represented the emotions I didn't want to feel, my shadow thrived on guilt, shame, and all the negative aspects about myself that I spent time suppressing. Both would involuntarily burst out now and then when I didn't expect them, or in periods of trauma or crisis. Trying to keep my shadow hidden was exhausting. I had no idea how to leverage its power for my own healthy use.

Like a set of weights I hadn't trained to lift, I hadn't built my emotional muscle over the years. Meantime, my shadow grew to ghastly proportions. There was little wonder that together they exploded unbridled into severe depression.

There was more from my past than my Beth and teen years that I needed to face. Although I was still struggling with the negatives and positives about myself as a mother, my exploration had skipped a critical period between my teens and motherhood.

A jarring nightmare provoked me to examine my early twenties.

> *Excerpt Ten*
>
> I dream that I'm standing alone in a room when something from the ceiling jumps on my back—a gray, amorphous, shadowy figure. Its sharp claws are digging into my flesh. I fight it off and see drops of my blood spattered across the walls. I turn to face this shadowy figure, and it morphs into an ugly version of my twenty-ish self.

I couldn't get the night terror out of my mind and discussed it with Katharina. She suggested I plunge further into the symbolic dreamscape and talk to a coach she had used with a Jungian approach to dream interpretation. Her coach had explained that, like poetry, the cryptic imagery offers hidden insights. Dreams allow us to process, guide, or call attention to issues in ways that bypass the ego.

That seemed plausible. Growing up, my family sometimes shared our nighttime dreams, speculating what they might mean. We knew well the Biblical story where Joseph's talent for dream interpretation helped the Pharaoh understand his prediction of seven years of plenty and famine. Maybe this nightmare was my unconscious screaming for attention. I was curious to learn more about how decoding nocturnal messages could help me.

Through working with the coach, I understood the creepy apparition was my shadow self, representing the "worst aspects of me." I also realized the ghoul was something I must transform, embrace, and merge into my whole. This particular spooky shadow represented the two years of my life with my former boyfriend, Frank, that I had previously tried to erase. In my early twenties, I had ripped from my journal and burned the pages detailing my time with Frank. Not long afterward, I had stopped writing in journals altogether, to ensure there would be no evidence of any future flaws. I also went through a religious process of confession and repentance about my sins with Frank, and it seemed to absolve my religious guilt. After ending the relationship, I hadn't kept my choices a secret among close friends and family, so it was not a hidden kind of shame. I still had baggage, though. It continued making me feel like a bad person.

I had been mortified, so I wanted to wish the relationship away. I didn't like what it represented about me. But burning my journal pages did not incinerate the shame and guilt.

There lingered a horrible proclamation of my capacity to justify myself into adverse decisions. It was not simply what I did, but also the how and why. While it had made me less judgmental of others (e.g. never say never), there was my propagandizer jeering, "What other horrible things are you capable of doing that you would never think possible?"

It was like believing the core of myself is solid stone, and then discovering it's permeable, porous, and easily crushed—not the unyielding rock I thought it was. "When I am capable of such self-deception, how do I trust myself?"

At the time, I blamed Frank for all the decisions I'd made and regretted. Now, I hadn't seen Frank in over thirty years. I had tried to erase him from my conscious memory. It didn't work consciously or unconsciously. It was only through facing myself that I could release the negativity lurking in the shadows. I resolved to reconstruct those two years by writing journal entries of everything I could recall.

Tackling this time period would require me to confront every aspect of myself, from virtue to vice.

Good and Evil

Everyone has
Good

And

Everyone has
Evil

It is only
the proportion
and perspective
that differ.

I spent a week writing about key events from that time frame. Here are some behind-the-scenes selections.

Excerpt Eleven

We met dancing in 1981 at a disco for the under-twenty-one crowd. Frank was a few years older than I was. He was a good dancer, and he dressed well. He was outgoing and gregarious. I was still nineteen, and the thought of faking my age to go somewhere to dance and drink never entered my mind—at least not yet. With his pronounced east-coast accent and fast-talking air of confidence, he was already different, and it piqued my interest.

Frank moved to a different apartment a few months after we met. I remember that he never quite unpacked his boxes, and his apartment was so disorderly. A part of him clearly needed help. Somebody for me to rescue, right? Exactly. I felt *needed*.

I remember buying some sheets for his bed at his new apartment and sewing a scallop in blue thread across the top of the white sheets to make it a more personalized gift. I didn't imagine that I would lose my virginity on those sheets. What a birthday present to give away.

Afterward, I remember feeling physically uncomfortable, and emotionally I proclaimed myself a horrible sinner. As an unmarried woman, I had committed one of the most egregious evils in the world—just short of murder—according to the doctrine that I followed then.

Frank talked about visiting New Jersey and New York, places he was very familiar with, as he had grown up there. I had saved money for a different trip that fell through, so I decided to apply some of my savings to a trip with Frank.

We stayed in New Jersey with his family and went to New York on the train frequently. New York was exciting, busy, noisy, chaotic, and dirty. In fact, for a long time, the smell of garbage reminded me of New York because the garbage workers union had gone on strike.

I found out it's true that "The City never sleeps," because one night, neither did we. I had been careful to get travelers checks for our trip. I would take enough checks with us for the day and then leave the rest safely where we were staying. This was before ATMs. I was worried about muggings.

This particular day, Frank exhausted the remainder of our daily budget by buying a polo shirt. We didn't have enough money to take the return train ride to New Jersey. Unfortunately, the store had closed by the time I realized this, and we couldn't get a refund. We were stuck in Manhattan with no money and no way to return to New Jersey. We walked the streets that night exploring. Finally, we ended up in Grand Central Station, napping for a while, sitting on the floor, and propping ourselves up against the wall, like homeless people.

We couldn't sleep on any benches in the parks or in the station because they had long since been equipped with dividers so that homeless people couldn't lie down on them.

We thought that we would return his new shirt and get our money back in the morning so we could take the train, but we were so exhausted that when the first train to New Jersey pulled out from the station, we were on it, without any tickets.

When the conductor asked for our tickets, Frank told him we didn't have any money because somebody mugged us. I was uncomfortable with this lie, but Frank was very smooth, and, apparently, our haggard looks were convincing. I had surrendered my financial comfort to him that day, but it wasn't the last time.

I had always been good at saving money, and he often asked me to lend him money, even though he was usually making far more at his job than I was. Sometimes he would pay me back part of what he borrowed.

By the time I ended the relationship, he still owed me $1,300. That was the equivalent of three months' wages from my part-time job while I was attending the university. I capitulated repeatedly, undermined my own sense of financial security to assist him, mimicked his spending habits, depleted my savings, and went into credit-card debt.

One night when Frank and I were on the dance floor, he made a comment about an attractive girl that passed by. Frank liked to clown around and exaggerate his movements. So, in this instance, he turned his whole head and body while he almost shouted, "Whoa."

Usually, when he did things like that, I would laugh it off, though it would sting me inside. This night, I decided to give him a light slap to play along with him, while hoping simultaneously to remind him he was with his girlfriend and shouldn't be acting like that.

As my left hand rose to give him the light, playful smack, I became enraged. My unexpressed aggression had built up from all sorts of other things unrelated to this particular episode, and I slapped him so hard that my watch flew off my wrist and shattered into pieces on the dance floor.

I stormed out of the building and went outside, infuriated and sobbing. I was shocked at my capacity for wrath and violence. This was an aspect of myself I did not think existed. I hadn't felt in control.

Over time, we migrated to a private disco that required membership because they served alcohol. I wasn't yet twenty-one, but I doctored an official-looking ID with my photo and a modified birthdate to get a membership pass.

This was a double whammy in the sin department. Not only had I lied to gain membership but I was also now drinking—another immoral act against my childhood religion. Sex, lies, rage, and alcohol—these were not what I expected of myself. I felt ashamed.

Writing about Frank was therapeutic. As part of reconstructing my twenty-year-old self, I thought about beneficial features of the time I dated Frank that I still cherish today. Most significantly, I met Gillis. I also bonded with Layla through Frank.

Gillis and Layla knew me during and after my relationship with Frank. They knew all the poor choices I made then and still loved me. Since they continued to love me, I wondered, "Why couldn't I love myself?"

I knew I was the one judging myself the most harshly. I reached out again to my siblings. I acknowledged some of the notions that I had held onto. We reminisced so I could recapture some of what I had forgotten. I went through every scrap of paper I could find from my childhood.

I allowed myself to feel Mom's abandonment. I remembered the home's hollowness. I had wanted to have Mom there to greet me when I returned from school, but it didn't happen until she retired early, in her mid-fifties, and I was already in high school. Aside from her full-time job, she spent many evenings performing in plays and working as a volunteer.

I had planned to work only part time when my children were school age so I would be home when they came through the door. They wouldn't be alone.

Part of my motherhood guilt was that I did not do this. I felt guilty somehow that I was not protecting my Beth self, either. I thought I knew where the guilt was coming from, but it would take another year before I fully realized the depth from which that profound emotion emanated. After writing the first draft of this book, an emergent memory compelled me to include one more chapter.

Abandoning my own children by working was one of the stories I told myself. On the one hand, I was beating myself up over these narratives. On the other hand, there were the recollections from my time with Frank, and all those emotions Beth had, that I didn't want to resurface or acknowledge.

"Why don't I trust myself?" I pondered. It was fear I chose— fear over love—because I felt it more strongly. It was not an actual choice because it took hold of me in a gripping way. Fear I wasn't good enough. Fear I had failed. Fear I could not go on. Fear constricted my chest and made my breathing shallow. My heart raced with my thoughts jumping to the worst cases of all the imaginary scenarios.

I was living in fear of the future and shame of the past. I was barely in the present, only long enough to do the mundane work duties and to distract myself from the future and the past. The life I had lived haunted me. I also feared the life I wanted would never materialize. It kept me awake, and it kept me oversleeping. It made my heart race but paralyzed my body—the contradictions of body, thoughts, and actions. I gained weight. It reinforced my negative self-image. I didn't like myself.

I tell you these aspects of my journey because although you have your own concerns, the journey is similar for all of us. The circumstances differ.

The few people I shared parts of my journey with before publishing this book told me they saw courage and strength in me. I didn't feel that way at the time. You have your own courage and strength even if you don't feel that way, either. You have made your way through other issues in your life. You will make your way through more.

The frozen layers thawed as I practiced swimming in the lake of emotion Beth had created. I no longer feared drowning. I had lifelines of friends, family, books, and other methods I used to get me through the emotional strokes. One of my tools was Robert Augustus Masters's audiobook, *Knowing Your Shadow: Becoming Intimate with All that You Are* (Sounds True, 2012).

Usually, when I would read self-help books, I would quickly scan through and skip the exercises, promising myself I'd come back to them. I didn't do that this time. I had enough motivation to write out what I was directed to ponder and answer. I listened to both the healing and terrifying words that formed in my head.

Following Masters's exercises, I did some activities designed to connect with my shadow self. I talked to myself and changed chairs to disparage myself as my propagandizer. I shouted at myself then took the other side to answer my accuser. I was the prosecutor, the victim, and the defense counsel all wrapped into one—three different spaces in the form of chairs to act it out alone.

I made myself vulnerable and uncomfortable in the process. I faced things about myself and divulged only to a trusted few. I wrote and journaled more about the shame and guilt. I allowed myself to feel the hurt.

I wrote a response to one of the questions that Masters's audiobook guided me through.

> *Excerpt Twelve*
> Thinking about the past, when I shut down feeling. It seems I stopped really loving myself. Guilt, shame, and shutting down emotions also shut down self-love.
>
> Is it connected to passion in this way: that I will again feel helpless lying on the bed? That to *feel* is to *feel the helplessness?*
>
> I still deal with the emotional shrapnel and wounds, while healed are still scars, areas that

when pushed still trigger shutting down. That year in eighth grade was hard. I believe I was depressed...I think it's part of the fear of tapping into myself.

Then I couldn't do the nurse thing because the pain I felt from the patients was too overwhelming. It was depressing to me because I was repressing. The office didn't require me to feel.

I don't need or want it anymore... *I need to shift ME*, become clear about my deepest desires and passions, not hanging on to those that don't serve me positively, and stop being conflicted. I want harmony—and need this *within myself*.

In seeming response to what I had written, I had another frightening dream about my shadow that gave me the opportunity to encounter it in a new way.

Excerpt Thirteen

Two men are on a natural stone walkway that seems quite high up from the bottom. There are no railings. Below the walkway is dark, so it's not clear how far the bottom is from them.

The walkway is like a bridge. Immediately, I associate it with the Bridge of Khazad-dûm in *The Lord of the Rings* movie, where Gandolf falls into a deep chasm while fighting the Balrog demon, Durin's Bane, in the Mines of Moria.

One of the men is nearer the end at the right side of the bridge, while the other man is on the left, three-quarters of the way toward the other end of the bridge. The man on the right shoots lightning-like fire bolts out of his fingers as if he's a wizard. The wizard seems at first to be trying to hit the other man with the bolts. The wizard is saying something like,

"Sometimes you need to kill the good to make way for the great."

None of the bolts strike the man on the left, as he simply turns his body sideways and bends slightly backward with ease so that the bolts fly completely past him to the other side, as if he's Neo in *The Matrix* movie, dodging bullets in slow motion.

Then it seems it's not the man on the left that the wizard is trying to hit, but something beyond and unseen in the darkness on the other side, a menacing presence hiding in a dark cave.

When I awoke and contemplated this imagery, I peered into the darkness in my mind's eye. The "menacing presence" emerged from the darkness of the cave. As it came closer, I recognized its hideousness as my shadow. It changed to a repulsive reflection of me.

Instead of shunning her, I imagined a white healing light bathing my shadow with love and acceptance. As I showered her with shimmering rays, she transformed into a mirror image of me. I absorbed and integrated her within me. Then, the entire scene changed. The gloom lifted as if the sun rose to midday brightness. Beneath the bridge babbled a beautiful blue river. On either side of its banks teemed lush green vegetation and blossoming flowers. The cave at the end of the bridge was no longer a dark cavern but instead became a light-filled opening. Its back wall had disappeared and in its place stood a pathway.

By facing and embracing the worst aspects I had been rejecting, I opened a passageway to new possibilities. Perhaps I was making a new path from the good to the great.

From Myself

Swirling,
golden light
fills my head.

Glowing,
lighting
my deepest
shadows,

traveling
down
through my body.

Igniting
my power,
my better me,
God-self to be.

Calm and
persuasive,
I carry myself,
lifting the
veil of
fear,
doubt,
worry.

Trust myself.
Love myself.
From myself.

12
BEGINNING TO BLEND

I wondered, when did I learn to keep secrets?

I had danced with my dark side, but I wanted to probe beneath the shadowy exterior and strip the secrets she held. There were some deeds I had not dared to reveal, while other secrets I had told only to a select few. Why was I still reluctant? It was judgment. I had already judged myself, and it wasn't pretty. I still felt ashamed, and I wanted to keep them hidden.

I had dealt with my relationship with Frank and the choices I had made. That felt comforting. Yet, there was still more. To release this, I deliberately searched my mind for private pain and secrets. I would mainly focus on actions from my childhood that I was reluctant to tell people about and had spawned my shadow.

I wondered, "When did I learn to keep secrets?"

I searched back to any story from my childhood that made me feel uncomfortable. I spotlighted each scene in secluded sessions where I could picture those thoughts in an intentional way and illuminate my understanding of them.

Dragging them out of the recesses of my mind, I also penned them. I would allow myself to feel the pain they caused me. That was not easy. The recollections didn't come all together, either.

One by one, they popped in my head, such as the time I became a thief.

> *Excerpt Fourteen*
> So, the author said to think of a time when I was shamed as a child. I was in first grade and my boyfriend, Nathan, encouraged me to steal a bottle of pop with him from Ernie's market, one block from my house. I knew it was wrong. I did it, anyway.
> We went somewhere to hide and drink them. Someone found out—I think it was one of my sisters—and we had to take a nickel each to Ernie for the drinks and apologize for stealing. It was really hard.
> To feel the shame again, as the meditation directed, is to know that I beat myself up. My shame covers me in a blanket of judging my whole person to be bad, rather than just the act. I didn't steal like that again. The shame feeling is the same regardless of the act. I put myself down and beat myself up (no compassion) when I feel shame.

At times, unrelated events would conjure memories. I wrote each one down. After writing, I would reread my depiction of the event. I would think of myself at that age and consider what I would have known.

During exploration, additional memories surfaced. My earliest memory emerged as I continued clearing unacknowledged shame's last vestiges to fully blend.

ชวง

I imagine myself sitting on the living room love seat with its gray fabric, half-moon back, and circular seat. My honey brown hair, cropped pageboy style, is hanging straight against my plump cheeks. My face still shows its baby fat. I picture my current adult self sitting with three-year-old Beth. I ask her why she's been sobbing and can't catch her breath. She tells me, "Daddy spanked me. I must have said something he didn't like. He got mad all of a sudden, and it makes me feel sad."

She's telling me this between short, spasmed breaths. She's still sobbing. I put her head on my bosom. Beth takes a deep breath and relaxes. I ask her to describe the scene.

Dad has come home with candy after a long day's work in construction. He smells like sweat and sawdust. It's so familiar a scent, and Beth relishes the sawdust aroma. All the kids are clamoring for his attention as he tells them what he has for them—a treat. She hasn't had this candy before. It is a dark-brown oval covered with powdered sugar. He calls it horehound, one of his favorite hard tacks, and she associates its name with a dog. She picks her own piece and plops it in her mouth. After the sweetness of the sugar dissolves, a horrible sulfur and molasses mix touches her tongue. She spits it out, repulsed, complaining, "I don't like it at all." The words spew from her mouth before she can stop herself.

Dad feels rejected and unloved because she's scorned his sweet gesture. He swats Beth on her behind. It feels a wallop to her. To him, it is a tap to remind an ungrateful child to act graciously.

Her siblings are staring at her while sucking on their own sweets. The sting of the spank is nothing compared to the angst she feels at being the odd one out and Dad's rejection. She bawls and runs away to her tented blanket where she plays army men with her brother and the neighbor kids. There she hides, wallowing in her victimhood. Her vocal vomit has earned her rebuff.

Later, when Dad brings home another tasty treat that doesn't altogether please her, Beth doesn't let anyone see where she spits it out. She doesn't tell Dad she doesn't like cantaloupe with her delicious vanilla ice cream. Instead of allowing someone else to enjoy the fruit, she pretends she's eaten it. In stealth, she shoves the uneaten cantaloupe through the crack in the utility room door's threshold. She cannot express her displeasure or preference because she will be rejected. She doesn't want that. She swallows her thoughts and buries them in her chest.

This is what Beth tells me without words, because as soon as my image of her fades away, I realize that candy wrapped my first charade. This was when I learned to stash secrets.

৪০০৪

Meditation was something I knew I should do routinely, yet I resisted. I had been regularly meditating before moving from the US, and they felt like mental mini-vacations.

When I was at my most depressed, I didn't meditate. I avoided it because I didn't think I could quiet my propagandizer's contempt. I knew meditation is as helpful as physical exercise, but I found it challenging to motivate myself at either of those options until I started to confront, absorb, and blend my shadow.

Awareness is the first step, as they say, and it takes some practice to realize what it's like when the mind and body are relaxed. Working through my secrets and mixing my memories with empathy, I began to note the difference between the new calmness versus the stress I normally felt. I became aware of where my body ached when I was not relaxed and how its pain echoed emotions. I continued to immerse in feelings and liberate negativity about myself.

Meditation helped me to maintain the lasting effects of the exercises I did consciously, rewiring my self-compassion, and visualizing the healing I needed. I would say that prayer is the asking or the *talking* to the connection we all have with our source of inspiration, while meditation is the *listening* to intuitive guidance.

I loved that little child and her shameful secrets that sprouted my shadow. I wanted to hug her, and I imagined myself doing just that in some meditative moments.

In speaking with Kristine one day, I told her my insight, "I met my shadow. I met my shadow self and brought her towards the light. Now she doesn't scare me anymore. She was me, and I love her now."

⁊⁓

Every other year since our parents died, my sisters and I schedule a small reunion for ourselves. It is my year to choose the reunion location. I select Sedona, Arizona, hoping that the wonderful nature surrounding us will evoke positive feelings for me. As we walk along the main street, I see so many tourist attractions and trinkets that do not appeal to me. I decide I will purchase nothing. Then, I spot a photograph of a beam of light entering a natural hollow of crimson sandstone. It touches something in me. I buy it without hesitation.

Stirrings

juicy creativity flows
oozing from fingers
dripping in prose
casting soulful lures

beckoning open-hearted
pulsing petals unfolding
naked emotion imparted
veiled literary disrobing

resonance susceptible
touching stirring within
rejection impermeable
the contextually virgin

Later, when I begin writing this book, I imagine myself writing at a desk inside that photo. A sunny spotlight streams and shimmers its way to the rich, red earth below my feet. I feel so enveloped by its warmth, and comforted. My soul soaks in its nourishment.

This airy cavern symbolizes my desire to bathe in the light, although sometimes I am in the dark. There is an opportunity for both.

Something about the crimson earth also binds me to my new homeland. The rich earth in Nigeria is naturally red, and when the rainy season comes, the natural ochre of the clayish soil repaints the bottoms of buildings with splashes of reddish water. I find an element of solace and peace in red earth.

These restful images evoke sounds of birds cheeping and chirping their mating calls in a thick ocean of rustling green leaves. I feel the sun streaming on my skin as I inhale and exhale. My breath deepens as I draw in the air, expanding my stomach like a child with a big tummy. I fill an imaginary balloon that extends from my stomach to the ground beneath my feet, then exhale as I release my stress, pain, and fear.

These are special scenes of imagination and connection, natural settings, where my mind and heart relish relaxation.

Exhale

Tho my chest's tight
everything's all right

Take a deep breath
and exhale

all is well
all is well

Centering Mantra

Heart spirit within me
Loving boundlessly
Embracing unconditionally
Protecting appropriately

Ethereal nurturer
Constant comforter
Mindful soother

Caressing
Blending
Centering

Tranquility

Gently not quietly
Cresting crashing creaming waves
Chattering cheeping chirping birds
Wispy windy whispery leaves
Natural tranquility

Latent aspects of myself are beginning to blend. I establish a regular practice of mental mini-vacations with guided meditations and visualizations.

With newfound inspiration, I resume my search for passion and meaning.

CAREENING CAREER

In naked confusion, I wonder,

Who am I? What gives me value?

13

MEANINGFUL MENTOR

A gift that cultivated my core...

Although I had uncovered a new feeling of passion about human resources, I wondered what I loved most about it. How did it tap into my deepest passion? Was there something specific that would provide meaning for me? Others told me I'm talented at developing people, but how exactly did that make me different?

Earlier, in the deepest depths of my despair, I had told myself I was *not* good at developing people. I received wonderful emails from former staff, thanking me for my role in their careers, but their glowing words made me feel guilty that I should have done more.

Those accolades also served as a reminder that I wasn't doing enough with my current staff, either. I felt inadequate. The sense of people-development as a leader connected to my sense of self as a mother—developing my "work children."

When I wasn't busy berating myself into depression, I normally had a great sense of pride helping people gain insights—and courage to progress. However, I did not recognize it as anything other than an acquired aptitude.

After my shadow work, I resumed my search for passion. I didn't know what set me apart, so I reached out to Barbara, my last boss in the US, and asked her why she once told me I was "the best developer of people she'd ever worked with."

Barbara gave me great feedback. She said the way I approached development was to use three critical ingredients:

- Always looking to expand their capabilities to do other things
- Extending trust in them to do those other things
- Creating an empowering environment through coaching and shepherding to help them succeed.

Further, Barbara explained that through my example of how I approached development for my staff, I had challenged her to be a better people-developer.

"How would I have learned to do this?" I wondered.

I reflected on that question and realized my first boss, Marilyn, had modeled it for me. I was nineteen years old when I started working for Marilyn, and I left the company when I was twenty-eight years old. I had grown from a temporary word processor to a human resources manager. Marilyn, with her pageboy blonde hair and tireless work ethic, was my work mom.

Marilyn modeled this behavior with me—even when I outright refused a higher level of responsibility because I was so afraid of failure, of stepping outside my comfort zone. Marilyn was wise, though. She gave me assignments bit by bit so that within a short time I was performing all the duties of that new role.

That was a critical juncture for me. I unconsciously adopted her approach as my own. Just as Marilyn had trusted me, I had extended trust to my staff to take on more—and I was always looking for ways to improve and expand their capabilities. Helping people learn and grow wasn't just an ability. It was a gift that cultivated my core.

Cornucopia

The sage places a basket
Full in eager outstretched arms.

Yearning though she is,
The young woman believes
Self undeserving of the gift.
She returns cornucopia to the sage.

The sage is not deterred
And asks for help in
Tending the garden.

Novice though she is,
The young woman
Plants seeds,
Sprinkles water,
Feeds nutrients, and
Removes weeds.

The sage provides advice
And oversees daily duties
Of the expanding grove.

Diligent as she is,
The young woman
Increases her knowledge by
Study of nurture's art and science.

The sage sees a garden thrive,
many a harvest year
With bounty overflowing
The fruits of labor.

Experienced as she is
The maturing woman
Moves to further pastures and
Tills a garden of her own.

The now mature woman is grateful
And wishes to share the plenty.

Blessed as she is
The aging woman
Must find one who will
Also tend the garden with
As much care and concern.

The aging woman places a basket
Full in eager outstretched arms.

Yearning though she is,
The young woman believes
Self undeserving of the gift.
She returns cornucopia to the sage.

14
UNEMPLOYMENT UNEASE

The jobless undertow drenches me in waves of worthlessness...

We maneuver along the pothole-laden express road. I'm obsessing, again. "Why did I come to Nigeria? Why am I staying? It's just too hard. It shouldn't be so difficult. I've never been in this situation before—not like this." For the first time in twenty-five years, I am unemployed.

The rain pouring outside reflects my drowning spirit, as the windshield wiper blades clear the barrage away only to cascade again. Sinking into numbing depths, I allow the tropical shower to flow as my vicarious tears. We have someone else in the car with us, so I dam the water welling in my eyes and submerge in silent emotion.

We stop for something to eat. Gillis flashes his brilliant ivory smile, hoping to brighten my clouded disposition. He brings me something delicious from the buffet counter.

I declare, "I'm not hungry," and stare through the café window, watching the pools deepen.

I scheme in silence, "Maybe I can starve myself."

৪୦୧৪

I am in my second-deepest period of depression. This time, my family and my expectations of them is not the issue. It is about the career I had held onto so tightly in the busyness of the last three decades when I was utilizing aspects of passion I didn't acknowledge. This joblessness seems like a cruel trickster, snatching newfound passion from my embrace.

During the preceding two years, even when depression gripped me in its strongest grasp, I had been working. Busyness was always welcome then. Soon after disentangling from that despair, my employment contract finished.

Frustrated with the false starts in every job-hunting attempt, I don't know what to do next. I struggle to stay afloat while the jobless undertow drenches me in waves of worthlessness. I imagine myself in the distant future, still without a job, having depleted my entire stash of savings. My melancholy conclusion is when that bleak future arrives, I will cease the struggle and kill myself.

This is, of course, illogical self-talk. I know this is so when I record my private ponderings on paper, or when they bound around my head like so many reverberating bouncy balls in a crazy person's padded cell.

Killing myself isn't my immediate plan. It's the course I chart for my dismal future when the hope I'm clinging to evaporates along with the money. When my sense of self-worth anchored to my career identity is as depleted as my bank account, I will allow myself the grim prospect of becoming nothing at that point, too. I am failing again.

Net

Fear I'm falling.
Will you catch me?

That netting
you're building,

116

still weaving—
it's incomplete.

Too many gaps.
I don't trust it
to hold my weight
or any of late.

Suspend the net—
the one you're creating;
it's not the answer.

I want you
to see where I am,
to see my tightrope,
to see my precarious pose.

I want you
to be by my side,
to be my acrobatic partner,
to be my net.

Extend the net,
the one inside you,
it's always been there.

Fear I'm falling.
Will you catch me?

Earlier, motherhood malaise stripped my private persona bare
to the bone. Now, lingering joblessness ruptures my comfortable
career mask. Together, these personal and professional building
blocks shatter my precarious identity to rubble. In naked
confusion, I wonder, "Who am I? What gives me value?"

Deemed Value

Courted by many
Bridled by none
Engaged for a time
Search ambles on

Not for a soul mate
Yet long-term match
Of interests and talents
A professional catch

Organizations needing
Competencies here
Or developing EQ
Better leadership steer

Of people and profits
Revenues and cost cutting
Adding deemed value
Soft and hard accounting

Touching their lives
In direct or unintended ways
It's really all worth it
Deep soulful amaze

I had left Lagos, a city of over eighteen million residents, like New York. I returned to Enugu, a town the size of Albuquerque, where my in-laws live among nearly one million other inhabitants. At first, I welcomed the calmer atmosphere as a change of pace. Part of me wanted to have a bit of a gap between jobs. In the beginning, I was not too worried financially because I had savings.

I believed I had a good idea of what I wanted. I was tenacious and expanded my search to include opportunities in other countries. I scoured the web using creative keyword combinations for suitable openings.

Within a few months, I'd applied at hundreds of firms. When the jobs still didn't materialize, I became concerned. My job-hunting attempts for human resources roles were hitting a brick wall—every single attempt.

Power Through

Feels like failure
So I resist the next
Turn and twist
In this unknown path

Wondering if walking
Straight a bit more
Will reveal the
Results I so desire

Power through
It's what I do

Remove brush
Try harder to trek
Clearly, directly
Ahead of me

There's only more
Now exhausted
Discouraged and
Angry at myself

Power through
It's what I do

Conflicting thoughts
Push on or shift
Heart choices to make
Is any one wrong?

Outcome expectations
Fuel my disappointment
Should anything right
Be so incredibly hard?

Power through
It's what I do

Wrong or right is
My own judgment
A label not accepting
What is or can be

Consequences
Positive or not
Flitting around
Clouding intuition

Power through
It's what I do

The gap I had wished for continued longer than was comfortable. I was getting concerned. I had days and weeks when I felt okay, good, and great. I also had melancholy, blue, and depressing days. Unemployment surfaced feelings of failure, rejection, and insecurity.

Generally, this despair was not as profound as before. However, I had my moments. Initially, I switched to a different type of busyness. I devoured 5,000 pages of fiction in two weeks to distract and engulf myself in an imaginary world. Still, I was sinking.

Determined not to drown in desperation, I then made self-development my "job" to remove whatever blockage was holding me back. I kept myself busy, but this was not a busyness of distraction any longer. I wanted the hurt to go away, but I was determined to use it and not avoid it. I allowed myself to immerse in emotion this time. I practiced my strokes by latching onto anger I had not let myself feel before. I journaled about resentment, hopelessness, frustration, and all my feelings. I felt blocked.

I found that when I resisted these surging sensations, it made them stronger. If I acknowledged the sentiments, I waded through them faster. I allowed myself to wonder, write, and evaluate them objectively or through my tears, anguish, or misery. The waves persisted the more I resisted. I chose to dive in and use the surges to carry me forward.

With nothing motivating me to roll out of slumber, I often overslept. My dreams lingered in my morning memory, and I recalled their details with ease. My coach and I dove even deeper in our analysis than before. I supplemented the homework she assigned by researching and reading related books and articles.

My dreams indicated I would be doing something a bit different. This new work would be fulfilling and an authentic, relaxed approach. If I let go of expectations and let it flow, I would see capabilities beyond my current focus on human resources. I would be exploring different angles and new approaches to work with a creative aspect to them, combining conventional and non-conventional elements.

I translated this information to mean that I should explore leadership development. My thinking was not radically different. I was staying within the box that I thought would work best, and would not drift me too far away from human resources and my newly acknowledged passions.

You would think that when over 300 doors shut, I might have acted on my dreamy dispatches. I was trying to flow and allow things to unfold, but I felt compelled or obsessed to continue applying for human resources jobs and related positions.

15
REJECTION CONNECTION

I did not need someone else to define my worth...

I thought I was still following my passion, and that this "new way" would continue in the extended realm of human resources. I also concocted an idea of the perfect role and circumstances, not unlike the idyllic family I had imagined for myself. My ego wanted leadership roles, similar to positions I'd held in the past.

An unexpected jolt acted as a catalyst for me to begin shifting my search toward other ways of expressing passion.

I applied for the head of human resources at a Lagos-based organization. They liked me, and I had been through the complete interview process. The executive recruiting company extended a verbal offer. The next day, I was preparing all my questions and readying for the contract negotiations when the recruiter called and rescinded the offer.

The circumstances were vague, and the recruiters had difficulty explaining, but the company claimed I lied about something nebulous in my background. To me, it felt as though they had slimed me and accused me of some crime—where I had no idea what the actual charge was, and no access to the judge and jury.

The recruiters would not divulge details. Explaining they had never faced a dilemma like this, they professed sympathy to me and embarrassment about the situation. They hadn't even started their official reference checking, so there was no evidence as a basis for the company's decision.

If the company had changed their minds so quickly, couldn't they simply say that? This fabrication made it sound like some hazy breach of integrity on my part placing the company as my victim. How could that be when I felt they were the ones persecuting me?

My disappointment fueled a fierce ally.

Brother Anger

Brother Anger,
I acknowledge you.
Thanks for the action
you drive me to take
when in discomfort.

I've been too long
a companion of
Sister Sadness.
Ignoring, suppressing you,
then your dark twin comes.

Sister Sadness has gone away.
Brother Anger displaces her today.

I had in my hands a letter from Barbara, extolling my virtues and praising my work. That letter served as my private vindication that the company and recruiter had not seen. I cried every time I read and re-read Barbara's recommendation letter that day. Barbara loved me and appreciated the work I did for her. That was evident. That horrible company didn't know me. These were not woeful weeps but instead flowing fury.

I wrote about my anger.

Excerpt Fifteen

Since I have suppressed my feelings in the past, I want to write down the emotions I'm acknowledging...Worrying about this doesn't bring me closer to a solution...I, of course, have permission to *feel* angry—and if it drives me to action I wouldn't have taken otherwise, then it's served a useful purpose.

I suppose it serves a useful purpose, anyway. I realize that when I am angry, I cry as a release. I can be furious yelling, yet also crying. So, maybe I don't need to let this go, or ignore or distract it. Maybe I just need to say that I'm angry about it. Yeah, that feels right. Here goes.

I am angry that it feels like a big slap-in-the-face moment that I *lowered* my salary expectations so dramatically and then get bitch-slapped and fucked over. Yeah. That's victimization talking, and I totally acknowledge that.

I'm angry that the recruiter couldn't get details of the package up front. I'm angry that I started to get excited, planning everything about my move as early as next week, and was envisioning myself in this role—only to be trampled and spat on, metaphorically speaking. I am angry that there is no real way to defend myself, my honor, my reputation, to this smear campaign.

I'm angry that Gillis feels so angry—yeah, that it didn't affect just me, but it also affected his emotional state. I'm angry that they couldn't have done this ahead of time, and not make an offer in the first place.

I'm most angry, though, that I really don't know any specifics about what they think they know about me, and there's no way for me to rebut and defend myself.

I'm also angry that this may all be a ruse, and I'm getting all upset and taking it personally—when, in fact, they may have an unrelated reason for wanting to withdraw the offer and are just basically making shit up about me as an excuse. That just seems wicked.

I'm also angry that this pain in my right shoulder blade is back—the kind that goes with a cluster headache—and that I just feel like sleeping, but my mind keeps jumping around so I'm not properly resting. Damn them for that! There, another big, deep breath. I've said what I want to say.

I can't solve this problem, and worrying about it does no good in this case, but it makes me ruminate over these events and makes me feel bad. I choose to feel good and fine and content in my own value that doesn't involve the stupid company or recruiter or anyone else—or the job, for that matter. There. I dove into the angry feelings. I feel a bit lighter and a bit more relaxed.

As I embraced anger and allowed it to pass through me, I released it and realized it was no longer necessary to take the situation personally. I wrote my official response to the recruiter, asked them to consider my stellar recommendations, and requested they keep me in mind for other opportunities with different companies.

I did not need someone else to define my worth—my career value. I was then at peace about the situation.

Armed with this awareness, I relinquished my obsession with human resources roles and pursued consulting and general leadership opportunities.

I was almost ready to unearth a buried desire, but first I had more self-development work to do.

Follow Your Heart's Desire

Follow your heart's desire,
For wherever it leads you
It will not fail.

Follow your heart's desire,
For whenever dear ones disappoint,
It will not fail.

Follow your heart's desire,
For whenever you feel distraught,
You have not failed.

Follow your heart's desire,
For however you feel delight,
Mighty barriers shall fell.

Follow your heart's desire,
So that you will shine
As a light for others to tell.

Follow your heart's desire,
For wherever it leads you,
At home you will feel.

ROAD TO RENEWAL

Awareness is the first step, right?

Now, how do I stop the cycles and the woe?

16
ADDICTION AWARENESS

I believe we do have alcoholism issues...

we just didn't have the alcohol...

Ennui Dread

Swimming around the periphery
of that deep, dark chasm beckoning me

Who knew nothing would be
utterly exhausting numbingly

Head spinning at the wake
unstable, unbalanced way I make

Through the mundane of things
frustrated no occupation brings

Lying prostrate, I can see
eyes slowly close blindingly

Dreamily of what is not
awake and think what I ought

Momentarily shattered productivity
of otherwise self-imposed invalidity

Mentally immobilized ennui dread
Completely, totally in my head

S till unemployed, my personal development work leads me to a book that is essentially the standard on codependency, *Codependent No More: How to Stop Controlling Others and Start Caring for Yourself* by Melody Beattie (Hazelden Foundation, 1986, 1992). I recognize the term codependent, of course. However, my family is not alcoholic. I think it doesn't apply to me.

A relative encourages me to read the book, anyway, telling me about her own codependency journey. I believe it might be worth the effort. After all, I want to get rid of the misery. I am looking at lots of different ways to ensure that I disentangle what's blocking me. I download the e-book and begin reading. I highlight text on almost every page. There are so many parallels. How can it be that I did not investigate this earlier?

I read about codependency and its symptoms. Beattie accurately describes the roller-coaster ride of emotions, obsessively trying to rescue loved ones, and hinging my emotional state on their actions or inactions or reactions. I immediately connect with this author. She found a way to deal with it. She said I could, too. It seems possible that if this is a root cause, I can get some relief.

I ask myself, "Is a codependent person someone *addicted* to fixing or helping? Is that part of why I'm so good at fixing organizational issues where I'm not emotionally distraught *and* why I don't like *maintaining*? Do I *like* problems because I'm *addicted* to them?"

I read the various ways that codependent behavior manifests, and highlight the ones that most resonate with me, such as:

- Feel compelled to help people solve their problems
- Not sure what I want or need or minimize my wants and needs
- Feel empty and worthless when I don't have a problem to solve or someone to help
- Instantly shift my own priorities to assist in resolving a problem
- Feel angry, victimized, and unappreciated when that issue has become mine
- Blame myself for everything (except of course, when I'm blaming other people for my feeling angry, victimized, and unappreciated)
- Reject compliments or praise (feeling I don't deserve them)
- Have been a victim of abuse (e.g. sexual, physical, emotional, neglect, abandonment, or alcoholism)
- Feel like a victim
- Have a lot of "should have, could have, would have" that causes tremendous guilt (also known as rumination)
- Constantly trying to prove I'm good enough to be loved
- Repeatedly try to control events and people through various forms of manipulation such as guilt, advice-giving, and helplessness
- Busyness like workaholism so that I don't have to feel too much and tell myself things will improve in time
- Wonder why I feel like I'm going crazy
- Believe the stories and lies that I fabricate and tell myself
- Don't love myself

- Look to relationships with other people to provide my positive feelings
- Have difficulty expressing my emotions authentically (good at repressing feelings)

The list is longer, but I'm sure you get the point. I don't think I've underlined a book more than *Codependent No More* unless it was a textbook. Of course, I logically know I am focusing on things beyond my control, but it is harder to see how I am disempowering others when I think I am helpful.

I can clearly see that codependent thinking and behaviors have caused so much stress and problems in my life. I knew about enabling, and some of my other issues, but never connected all of them together at the root of codependency. My codependent nature has been to rescue without explicit requests, disempowering people who are perfectly capable of doing for themselves. Therefore, in my goal to help solve the problem, I create new ones.

Denominator

The actors change,
as do the scenes
of the deep, painful, ecstatic,
overwhelming, consuming,
dramatic performances.

I remain blameless.
I am static.
They need to change!
Why don't they shift?

The words differ,
scripted so cunningly.

We deceive ourselves thinking
change comes from another.

Divide the past parts as you will,
they are only variables
with a single constant.
I am the common denominator.

Okay, so I admit I am a codependent. Awareness is the first step, right? Now, how do I stop the cycles and the woe?

There's a series of twelve steps to the recovery process, but Beattie states it very simply. We are responsible only for ourselves. When we do for others what they can't do for themselves, that's healthy. However, when we do for others what they can do (and should do) for themselves, that's a codependency trait.

Key to Codependency

The key
Setting me free:
My responsibility—
Is only for me.

Being responsible only for me is both a frightening and liberating concept. I feel so accountable for much more than myself, and I want to resist Beattie's idea. At the same time, it gives me permission to begin enforcing my weak, porous, and non-existent boundaries.

୫୦୧ଓ

I eagerly continued reading *Codependent No More* and carefully did the exercises, not wanting to miss the opportunity for healing. With my newfound insight, I sought discussions with my siblings.

I told them I'm not looking to assign any blame; this is about understanding context.

We had and have a wonderful family in so many ways. Our family was also dysfunctional. I explained that I find it helpful to connect the dots and to see when patterns formed early on. I was seeing some critical parallels between my parents' relationship modeling and what I was repeating in my own marriage.

Mom and Dad had gone through family counseling when I was in elementary school. Because of the guidance, Mom had often told me, "You can't change someone's action; you can only change your reaction."

Most of the time, this was the advice she would invoke when I complained to her about Quintin picking on me. I didn't fully understand her statement. Even as an adult, I logically knew what she meant, but it wasn't easy to put it into practice, and I didn't keep it top of mind.

My parents had tried to rectify their dysfunction, but they didn't know a key factor until a few years before their deaths when a doctor diagnosed Dad with bipolar disorder. That diagnosis helped to explain so much of the underlying cause. Dad had struggled all his life with this condition without realizing he had it. When he received treatment, it was immediately effective.

My sister, Yvonne, put it this way: "I believe we do have alcoholism issues in our family of origin. We just didn't have the alcohol."

While still living in the US in 2010, I felt that through some months of self-development probing, meditating, and looking for healing, I had solved my problems. I hadn't. I certainly had insights, yet they were not enough. I couldn't or shouldn't say, "Okay, check that box. I'm cured. Self-development is done." However, that's exactly what I *did* say to myself. I was justifying not continuing the work I had started.

Shortly before I moved from the US, I had been continuously happy for months—the longest timeframe that I remembered. I had been shifting my perspective, and this brought a great amount of healing in the right direction. When I stopped the self-development activities, atrophy set in. I moved to Nigeria. I changed jobs twice. I wasn't in the same environment mentally and physically, and I wasn't maintaining the habits that provided a conducive state of mind. It was the emotional equivalent of losing weight on a fabulous diet, only to regain all the lost weight, plus more, when the old eating habits resumed.

I slipped into familiar patterns before realizing it, and as I relocated to Lagos—the second move in two years—I was more alone than ever, without family and friends nearby. Gillis was often gone for weeks at a time. It would be a stressor for anyone, but by that time, my emotional state had already eroded. I didn't need outside circumstances from my family to trigger much because my psyche was ripe for the picking. The result was I didn't live in the present and had a lot of time alone to fixate on the past and future. That was during my descent into despair.

There were other factors in this situation, too. For example, I did not continue my exercise regimen. While I was living in Arizona, I had been jogging two miles a day and meditating on a regular basis. I ceased jogging. I stopped meditating. The doctor diagnosed me with Hashimoto's thyroiditis, an autoimmune disease, shortly before I moved. However, all of these were peripheral and contributory to a perfect storm that engulfed me as my codependent disposition to rescue swelled.

Codependency is something passed from generation to generation. It is in my family of origin. It is in the family I created with Gillis.

I sought to open this disclosure for discourse. Could my own healing—and talking about my codependency—help Gillis and our adult children? Ha! I'm not responsible for them. No, I would not discuss codependency with them to *rescue* them from codependency. This would be an introduction—to create awareness and provide an opportunity for self-insight if they would like it. That's a different approach from my usual compulsion to rescue.

Yvonne was well versed in codependency. We discussed my insights, and I discovered that her own search had started some years prior. She had done a lot of studying and had worked through deep distress herself. This was fascinating. Yvonne also explained that she understood this was something she would deal with, to varying degrees, for the rest of her life. That was a critical point, I realized.

ജോ

I acknowledge now that personal growth is constantly evolving and never ending. As I become more authentic, those areas that still need healing continue to surface. I know I have the ability to break my cycles and shift in a lasting way…but only if I maintain my self-development in some form forever, and do not allow for complacency.

I will create and maintain proper boundaries. These will not be demarcations based on fear and anger but grounded in self-love and care.

Boundaries

Boundaries
undefended

Clarification
unrequested

Assumptions
conjectured

Blame
assigned

Anger
erupted

Victim
reaffirmed

Demarcation
staked

Request
expressed

Situation
stated

Intent
aligned

Paradigm
shifted

Power
Reclaimed

೮೦೦೮

While the idea that I am responsible only for me was liberating, I was troubled for a different reason. I wondered, "If my passion is helping other people pursue their passion and tap into their potential, how is that not living vicariously? Isn't that fixing or some form of rescuing? Since it's a codependent thing, now what? Do I have *any* passions that aren't shaped by my codependency?"

I explored and re-read portions of Beattie's book. I reminded myself that it is about the approach and the intention. If I am acting as a coach or mentor to guide another, it is not codependent. If I'm not obsessing about fixing the other person, but providing insight as my own coach had been doing, that is also not codependent.

I asked myself again, "What is my deepest desire?"

Before I read *The Artists Way*, it never consciously entered my mind to write, even when my son, Kenneth, was inspired to write an extensive collection of stories that would take several volumes when finally compiled. He studied the style and techniques of authors he admired. His handsome, thickly lashed brown eyes would stare intently at the computer for marathon hours, mapping his characters' features and their intersecting story lines. I marveled at and admired his creativity and persistence. I had no book burning to come out. Rather, I didn't *think* I did. Remember, I'm good at suppression. However, now that I had composed some poems, this was something to consider.

A few months passed. Barbara told me she'd written a book while encouraged by a writing coach, and then sent me information about his method and books. I obediently followed the coach's writing exercises. They were helpful to clear my fears. That wasn't the only thing clearing.

One book posed a question about my earliest memory, such as, "When was I first drawn to write?"

At first, I was in denial, thinking, "I've never had such a wish." Then, profound emotions surfaced and washed over me. I could deny no more.

As I journaled my reaction to the question, my story unfolded, and its contents stunned me. I couldn't believe I was writing about myself.

Excerpt Sixteen

I only remember wanting to be a nurse at an early age, but my heart tells me that as I began to explore the idea of writing, I wanted that from an

140

early age as well—age six—when I learned how to read. It was a marvelous world. But, apparently, this was a secret that I kept from myself.

It must be true, for when I read the author's own experience, I cried. I cried out loud and couldn't stop for a few minutes. I am *still* holding my hand over my mouth, and exhaling the shock and surprise that his words would slap my emotions like a backhand to my face.

Like him, I knew when I was six, too. What I don't know is where that went. Why did I bury it? That's unanswered, but maybe it will come as I write and heal.

That sounds reasonable. Perhaps it doesn't matter so much why or how, but only to know at last that I have held this deeply for a long time. Exhale. Yeah. Feels good. A release.

This is the menacing clown in my dream. I saw fear where joy should be, so I suppressed my desire to write.

Having been so cut off from my own emotions, I finally understood that this sudden surging emotional shockwave was my body's way of shouting a core truth to me. At last, I heard it. I discovered the precious jewel I sought for so long. It was not connected to anything cultured by codependency.

Writing was my sparkling prize to claim.

17
DELTOID DYSFUNCTION

She dangles an invisible hook of

victimhood to catch a rescuer...

I am at a women's association dinner with about forty other members. The woman sitting next to me, Delores, is complaining, "My drink has not been delivered by the waiter."

I commiserate with Delores about the poor service and reply, "I had a similar issue, so I went to the counter in the bar to get a bottle of water myself."

I notice that Delores has a cane lying on the floor next to her, so I assume she will probably not want to walk to the bar herself.

Practicing my new awareness about rescuing, I decide not to act on my assumption without confirmation.

I inquire, "Would you like me to go to the bar to get you a drink, as well?"

This way, I'm not acting without explicitly requesting permission first. I smile inside as I pat myself on the back about choosing my response.

However, Delores responds with a "No."

Her curt reply disappoints me, and my internal smile dissolves. I wish to avoid this deltoid game, but Delores wants to play it. I recall the dysfunctional three-role pattern of human behavior I had recently discovered. The original concept is the "drama triangle" by Stephen B. Karpman, M.D. The three players are the persecutor, the victim and the rescuer.

The object of the game is to be the victim, getting our needs met without asking directly. Rescuers rush to provide aid and solutions, although victims merely hint and whine about their problems. When victims feel supercharged, they flip to persecutors. They still believe they're suffering even though they have become bullies. The payoff in this conflict is getting ego needs met indirectly or discharging feelings.

In dysfunction, we each play all three of these roles, although we tend to play one more dominantly. We can play out this drama switching positions with other people—within the same interaction. We can also play all roles within our own head when our inner critic persecutes us. The drama escalates as we flip from one character to another. The faster the roles change in the game, the more intense the drama and emotion. It operates on a win-lose style of conflict resolution with either/or thinking that deteriorates to a lose-lose situation.

Although Delores is unaware of the triangle, I know it doesn't matter as long as I don't step into it with her. I also know this is normal; people often refuse the explicit attempts for help because they want to stay in the victim role.

I console myself that when Delores rejects my offer, she is not rejecting me. She intends to play this invisible game, and I should not worry about it or take it personally. I tell myself, "This is not my problem—not my responsibility." I don't want to play this game with Delores or shoulder her concern.

Delores continues to complain, however. Eventually, a server brings her soda. To her dismay, the soda bottle label clearly displays the word "diet," and Delores doesn't want it. She complains again to anyone who will listen. She dangles an invisible hook of victimhood to catch a rescuer. I can't resist the lure. I take the bait, and I'm hooked.

I forget my deltoid avoidance training and launch into rescue mode. Now shouldering her problem as if it were mine, I scan for solutions. A few seats down, another woman has the same brand of soda, but it's not a diet. This time, I don't ask Delores if she wants my assistance. It was a subconscious correction for her previous rejection of my explicit request.

I ask the woman on the other end, "Would you mind trading drinks?"

She says, "That's fine."

We trade.

I place the swapped soda in front of Delores. My inner smile returns as my dinner neighbor's problem disappears. I wait for a thank you. Delores doesn't thank me, however. Again, she lodges a complaint.

She touches the soda bottle and proclaims, "This is too warm."

The soda I've swapped is not cold enough for her.

Her problem jabs deeper below my skin. The load I carry on her behalf feels heavier. I don't want to keep it. Indignation rises from my chest as my back burns with her burden. I prepare to hurl her problem at her, maybe even whack her with it. As my mouth opens, preparing to pepper Delores with biting remarks about how ungrateful she is, I realize my mistake.

Delores *wants* to stay in her victim role.

She hadn't given me permission to help, and I didn't explicitly ask this time. She reeled me into the drama triangle. I fell for it with my rescuer compulsion. If I were to express resentment, I would still be playing the game. She would remain the victim, but I would become her persecutor.

My lips trap the unspoken barbs with a quick inhale. Inner ire ebbs and forms a silent chuckle. I step away from the triangulation, making no effort to fix her latest problem. My deltoid load lifts.

I conclude that if it's important to Delores, she is fully capable of solving her own problem. Eventually, Delores gets the server to bring a soda cold enough for her to enjoy.

ഇറയ

It's a minor situation with a new acquaintance, yet it demonstrates how we—as compulsive rescuers—let ourselves get sucked into problems that aren't ours in the first place and no one overtly asked us to solve.

I contemplated, "Why would Delores's rejection rile me so much? When the dysfunctional interactions involve friends, children, spouses, parents, or siblings, shouldn't that be more emotional?"

People we love can trigger intense feelings of vulnerability and heartache through established patterns of unhealthy behavior. However, even strangers can play a fierce drama game. The emotions in one situation—seemingly unrelated—trigger deeper emotions from earlier events and trauma. Wilder Penfield, a neurosurgeon, discovered in his research that everything in our conscious awareness is recorded in detail and stored in the brain. Whenever current feelings match a memory, they are capable of being "played back" in the present. Delores's rebuff had surfaced my past feelings of rejection.

After the encounter with Delores, I re-read about the drama triangle. I noted three behaviors most problematic for me:

- Consistently doing more than my fair share of the work in helping (but not realizing it in the moment…that pillow analogy)
- Not asking for what I need and instead focusing on others' needs
- Trying to help or meet others' needs without being asked, or without explicit permission or request (this

excludes legitimate acts of kindness and compassion where others can't do for themselves)

The key to stepping out of the skirmish is to ask before attempting to help a capable person. Otherwise, it is rescuing. I can't say that I always ask for permission before I offer solutions, but whenever I become conscious of the dynamic, I do. For transparency, I have also explained the idea to my family and friends.

It shifts interpersonal interactions. I'm not trying to change them. I'm changing myself. Mom was right. I can choose conscious responses instead of automatic reactions. This is helping my journey to well-being and providing a better sense of mental health. Most of all, it assists with unraveling my rescuer addiction.

It is a stunningly simple and elegant model that explains dysfunctional interpersonal dynamics so well, yet manifests in such complicated interactions because relationships are flipping among the three positions and escalating the drama.

Practicing what I've learned about codependency and the drama triangle, I began to feel empowered.

18
GRATITUDE WITH ATTITUDE

Today, I am grateful for...

While personally I was feeling better, professionally I still felt stuck. Unemployment continued. Another of Beattie's books (*Make Miracles in Forty Days: Turning What You Have into What You Want,* Simon and Schuster, 2010) recommended keeping a gratitude log—especially when you don't feel grateful. Previously, I tried to express gratitude using a different approach, but I was feeling anger, disappointment, and despair. I didn't continue.

However, Beattie said to write, "Today, I am grateful for..." and then list a few things that pop into your head, based on how you *feel* about them. They don't have to be positive. They can be negative. I doubted its effectiveness, but it gave me permission to cling to my bad attitude while exploring gratitude.

Fighting Antipathy

I've a hidden disability
disguised from the outside
it isn't at all physical
but mental parts inside.

It isn't always present
crops up from time to time.
So maybe disability isn't
what to claim as mine.

Illness may be better apt
yet not always that ill
tho' underlying malaise lingers
even when happiness I feel.

Try to be in the moment
and with gratitude I seek
to focus on more positives
than negatives making weak.

My own source of medicine
like little anti-bodies fighting
against self-antipathy and
darkness growing, gnawing.

Exposing, naming curatives,
small doses to present,
and immersing in the moment
relieve unease like heaven sent.

I still had rough days, but I captured their unsuppressed emotions and processed through them more quickly. I began to have genuine gratitude. Here are some notes from my second gratitude log. Some of them sound like I'm complaining. I am.

> *Gratitude Notes*
> *Day 8: Today, I am grateful for...*
> I don't really know where the days go. I feel like I should be more productive. All these projects around me, still waiting to be done.

Day 9: Today, I am grateful for...
I went twenty laps walking around the compound.
I have that anxious feeling again. I want to cry.

Day 10: Today, I am grateful for...
I feel more hopeful today and glad that I was able
to shift that inner critic that overwhelmed me
yesterday morning. I did some shadow/self-critic
meditations yesterday, too. Glad I didn't stay
sucked in.

Day 13: Today, I am grateful for...
I feel I've turned a corner on so much emotional
baggage I didn't realize was there—I have made
connections and processed through. Now
working on my rewiring.

I'm really grateful for my family, and that I feel so
much more comfortable in accepting what is, and
building individual relationships.

Day 28: Today, I am grateful for...
I had a major meltdown, and my propagandizer
told me again how worthless I am and that I'll run
out of money and should just kill myself.

I had great discussions with Yvonne and Katharina
about my codependency issues.

Day 30: Today, I am grateful for...
I feel I have clarity and a way forward to untangle
myself from the worst aspect of my
codependency, even though I stayed up till nearly
three AM to do it. As I wrote out the issue, I
came to have peace with it.

Day 39: Today, I am grateful for...
I am so incredibly thankful for this miracle I prayed for and started writing this gratitude journal about...I didn't think something like this could happen now.

Gratitude Attitude

To get more
of the same
have a
gratitude attitude

The secret
they say
start small.
There is life
maybe health
nature gives
each and every day

Flowers open
birds chirp
sun shines
dog tail wags
kitty cat purrs
drink it in
feels like wealth

Intangible
cannot measure
ever present
only to notice
if you're present
in the moment

Perspective
is the view
that you choose
and none other
Expand your view
beyond nature

Every day
just a few
take note
what you have
not what you don't

Becomes a habit
and engrained
Then the attitude
will be filled
with gratitude

Come what may
not always easy
but let the negative
go its own way

And refocus
on your pleasure
every day
just a few
in your attitude
gratitude

The instructions include that at the beginning of the forty-day gratitude cycle, you record something miraculous that you want to happen. Then you write a daily gratitude log. Sometimes it takes more than forty days, so you continue with the next cycle.

My miracle materialized in the second forty-day period. I had longed for it more than seven years.

I don't know how the gratitude log operates. Perhaps science will explain how setting an unattainable, miraculous goal—while we focus on searching for gratitude—works. Science already validates that you don't actually have to *be* grateful for what you write in a gratitude log. Alex Korb, Ph.D., is a neuroscientist and author of *The Upward Spiral: Using Neuroscience to Reverse the Course of Depression, One Small Change at a Time.* He explains research and techniques about habits that can cultivate happiness. Searching for gratitude is one of them. Sure, it helps if we're actually grateful, but it's not required. The mere act of searching for gratitude increases serotonin production in the anterior cingulate cortex.

I had finally gone through all five stages of grieving the loss of my wished-for flawless family. Instead of repeatedly cycling through the first four stages of denial, anger, bargaining, and depression, I arrived at acceptance, the fifth stage. I surrendered to the idea that there may never be a shift in the family dynamics, as I had idealized. Then my family miracle happened.

I was ready for a personal miracle of self-forgiveness. That would require action on my part, not just a gratitude log.

Saltiest sea
lifts me
buoyantly

Flow
Float
Relax

Recline in
the brine

Surrender

19

COMPASSIONATE COMPANION

By forgiving others, I also forgave myself...

G etting in touch with anger was crucial. Finding a way to release it was more important. Anger takes a deep root, so we must dig deeper than we planted it. I found the process of forgiving myself far harder than letting go of other people's hurtful actions.

Excerpt Seventeen

In terms of self-forgiveness, what do I honestly expect is possible? It's simple—and yet not so easy to unwind the internal propaganda of my own mind. Self-care, compassion, responsibility...well, responsibility is the key right there—being responsible for *myself*, *my* compassion, *my* forgiveness, *my* self-love.

I fear it won't last—yet, I hope this is my final key to unlocking me. I expect that this, combined with all the other work I've done, will give me the ability to maintain what it is I need.

I also found it required multiple attempts in some cases before I was able to take out the taproot of the anger tree and let it heal with forgiveness. I still find saplings growing where I thought I had removed the mighty oak of my discomfort and pain. Those are easier to remove nowadays. They are not as tormenting. They haven't been growing as long. They don't require as much darkness as the oak did. They don't have as many branches or other trees sprouting from them.

As The Acorn Grows

As the acorn grows
Into the mighty oak,
My acorns now splendidly
Tall and majestic,
Are nearly ready to spread
Acorns of their own.

And so it goes,
As it has before,
Expanding the mighty forest.

No longer the child of my fore parents,
Nor the parent of your childhood,
We meet as adults discovering
Roots leading to behavioral boughs,
Protective bark, and
Creating our branches of genealogy.

I continued to write down my dreams on a daily basis. Experiences I thought were long forgotten and may have been suppressed or repressed would play out in ways that my mind and ego could not prevent in my slumber. I looked at the recurring dream themes as my cue on what to focus on.

I wrote about my woes. I penned my forgiveness of others. I again wrote as much as I could remember about situations that seemed long forgotten, but tucked away—first peeling the bark to expose the trunk, examining branches, limb by limb as they came to awareness. I practiced the exercises and read the book, *The Power of Self-Forgiveness: Treating Yourself with the Love & Respect That You Might Not Know You Deserve* by Thom Rutledge (New Harbinger Publications, 2012).

I went to the taproot. I talked to myself, as I had done for my earlier shadow work. It was important to speak aloud—and at times shout—when nobody could hear or answer except my shadow and me. My shadow, while better integrated, still needed forgiveness. I had made progress blending that aspect of myself I call Beth. The next step on the journey was to heal my shadow through forgiveness.

I meditated on my feelings. I noticed how I felt and where in my body I experienced the anger and the pain. I allowed myself to relive what I could, as I felt able. I didn't want to overwhelm myself with emotion again and fall into deep depression. I dredged up memories and allowed them to emerge over several months' time—not over a few days or weeks.

I read again through my journals. I looked at historical evidence prompting conscious recollection. I was in denial about some issues. This is when a coach or counselor is a great interventionist. They see objectively.

My coach pushed and nudged me. It was her role. She could see things I couldn't—the landscape of my forest where the oaks, merely pruned, remained. She helped me to explore the forest, see the trees, and come out of it with more compassion for myself.

I had gone through extreme guilt and shame as part of my severe depression in 2012 and 2013, and those thoughts had not completely gone away. I still had to confront them to come back to my loving self, loving me.

Your Answer

Tornadoes of fear swirl,
laying waste to swaths
of fertile possibilities.

Calm the mental winds.
Take shelter in the heart.
Sow seeds of self-love.

Your answer roots in soul.
Nurtured in gentle breezes,
blooms unknown knowing.

Forgiveness of ourselves isn't easy. We have a hard time looking in the mirror to acknowledge our actions and inactions. Sometimes, it's as if someone else's life plays in my mind. Denial. Acceptance. Forgiveness.

I named specific incidents that caused me agony and anger. I wrote them out in as much detail as I could remember. I then went through a second process after I had written every name and situation still painful to me. I reviewed them one by one—identifying how each had affected me, and what learnings I had from it—and began to shift my perspective to a loving and forgiving one. I wrote my forgiveness of each person. Then I said aloud the forgiveness I extended to each individual. By forgiving others, I also forgave myself.

In many instances, the pain and anger occurred because I did not enforce my boundaries—thin though they might have been. I know there were so many times when I could have pointed the finger and placed the blame, the shame, at others. However, it was mine to own, too. That's the tricky part. The anger I felt and the forgiveness I was re-extending, also needed to extend to myself. It was easier to forgive others than to forgive myself.

One of my favorite exercises from Rutledge's book was this one: He says to write down the negative and positive thoughts you have about yourself in two different colors of pens—one color representing the positive thoughts and the other color the negative ones.

I did two exercises like this. The first exercise was to focus on good things about myself. As soon as I started writing down the good notions, I would have negative thoughts. I wrote the negatives in red ink. When I tried to focus on the good about me, my inner critic was saying *but*—and then the rest of the text was negative. I wrote it down, anyway.

The second exercise was to focus first on the negative things about myself. I wrote the negatives in red, and then my inner propagandizer would be silenced, allowing the voice of reason to say *but...* The rest of the text was then positive, so I wrote it in black ink.

These exercises were giving voice, allowing me to hear the negative, and not suppressing it. Because I was not suppressing, it actually went away faster without trying. Moving through the misery wasn't easy, but it was necessary.

I wrote things that bothered me about myself. I transcribed taunts from my incessant propagandizer. I wrote down the internal chatter one by one. I noted how horrible I was, what a bad mother I was—and my list of reasons why that was still true.

As I let them flow, I had to change the pen to start the "but" about the parts that I liked about myself. As I allowed myself to focus on the negatives, my mind would switch to the positives.

Here are three examples of writing the positives first. Negative thoughts are bolded for differentiation.

My hair is long, full, and pretty **except that it's dry and poufy and needs to be trimmed.**

I have done a good job adjusting to Nigeria **except that I still feel insecure and talk about leaving and nearly died a couple of years ago, but that wasn't just about being here, so stop that.**

I have a talent with developing people—my staff—**so why can't I do that for myself and for my kids? Who am I kidding? I wasn't even all that great for my staff. They praise me because they don't know any better—they've had really shitty other bosses.**

Here are two examples of writing the negatives first:

I'm never going to get a job. But this is the longest I've gone because I always have had a job, except a couple of times, and it's normal at my level for some time to pass. It's not a reflection on me—it's not personal. I've had interviews and referrals. I'm up for a few jobs right now.

This self-development is never going to bring lasting change but I have the power within myself, and it's all up to me and nobody else about how I feel and what I do. So I can choose, and make the effort to keep on for the rest of my life…and little setbacks don't define me as a failure—they are *normal.* Everything is a learning opportunity—*everything.* So, there is no bad in it unless I judge it to be so.

Truth

In the stillness
of the night,

I hear my voice
Inside talking—

Nothing to drown
distract, disturb.

I hear clearly.

It must be lonely,
my voice.

I shut it out
willfully.

Not willing to hear
what it beckons

me to see with
eyes closed,

deep within,
resonating

to the core,
my own truth.

My family and friends loved me when I didn't love myself. Then, through self-forgiveness, I found a priceless treasure: my own self-love. That is the new tree. It is bright, strong, and straight. It grows rapidly—amazingly so—in the sun. Not an anger tree, but a tree of love, self-love.

There's no rewriting my history. It is a part of me, and I am now at peace with it. I have significantly reduced the enormous self-judgment I've carried all these years. I have come to terms with the difficult periods of my life. If I could have acted any differently, I would have. All of this is part of the duality in nature. No more could have, would have, or should have. I did have some fun times. I had some terrible times. It was life.

So, I think it appropriate to be thankful–no...*grateful*–for the two painful years I wanted to erase while with Frank, what he represented as an unwitting teacher, and what I learned. I have enormous strength and resilience. Everyone makes mistakes he or she wishes to undo, but casting them aside, suppressing them, continuing to be ashamed, believing they make us less of a person, striving for perfection—these do not serve our purpose.

I smile as I sit here and reflect, rather than ruminate. I see how events in life build and teach us, helping us prepare for other challenges down the road. I view the people I had difficulty with as merely representing many teachers in my life, catalysts, and a part of the duality in nature. Now, setting aside the self-condemnation and skewed perspective, I can finally acknowledge that the tapestry life weaves strengthens us. Everything is an opportunity to learn and grow. I instantly have genuine compassion for myself. With tears in my eyes and a little smile on my face, I nod my head and say to myself, "All is well." Then I write in my journal.

Excerpt Eighteen

Beth, I am sorry to have discarded you, believing you were not important, not worthy of attention, not something I should take along on my journey. I rejected you, a part of myself. I would not identify with you. And now that we're together again, I hold you in my arms, embrace you, and tell you with my most warm and heartfelt self that I love you. I love we. I love me.

Together, we can be called whatever we want. The name was merely a symptom or mask. It no longer matters. What matters is that we are one—all together again. Sigh. Deep breath. Release. Smile—a Mona Lisa-type smile.

20
DIVINE DEVOTION

Allow the unfolding, divine whispers hear...

๛ 2015 ๛

After self-love further bonded my Beth and Liz selves, my exploration took me to another place I needed to re-examine. There was a question in *Codependent No More*, "When did you take away the power from the higher power? When did you decide essentially that you had to take control of everything?"

I revisited and pondered that question. I had rejected the dogma of my childhood religion. That had happened sometime in my twenties. The problem was that I had not landed on a replacement. Sure, I had joined another church and attended services. I had been a Sunday school teacher for ten years.

I hadn't bothered to dig too deep to replace the religious doctrine of my youth with spirituality within my own comfort zone. I knew for sure what I no longer believed. I was not certain what I currently believed.

Yvonne had also left our childhood religion and joined another congregation that allowed her the freedom to worship a God of love that she saw reflected in scriptures. I had a conversation with Yvonne while we were discussing codependency, and she asked me, "What was the trigger or catalyst that caused you to disconnect from our childhood religion?"

I couldn't recall at that time what my experience was. Was the disengagement gradual? I wondered if there had been any particular catalyst. I knew I had apparently made the break by the time Victoria and Kenneth were born, and I was twenty-five.

A God of rules was my indoctrination. If you follow the rules, you get God's love. That also translated to obedience earning my parents' love as well. I had wanted to know all the rules to follow. Now, I unwound from that dogma and their rules. I wanted a much broader view. I was determined not to bind myself again in the way that religion had conditioned me to believe.

When Gillis and I met, I insisted that he convert to my religion as a prerequisite to marriage. He acquiesced. To him, he was changing from one Christian denomination to another, but it was vital to me.

However, within a year after we married, he became disillusioned with the doctrine and the way people were practicing it. There were many inconsistencies in his understanding of Christianity and my congregation's teachings. There was also a pervasive culture of racial prejudice. Parishioners' behavior reflected discriminatory remnants of official and unofficial tenets.

Gillis decided he would not continue attending my church. We had heated arguments about religion. We disagreed on so many points, neither of us yielding or considering the other person's point of view. It was a painful time for us, but I privately hoped he would change his mind and return later. Our resolution was to agree we would never divorce over religion.

Slowly, over the next couple of years after our agreement, I expanded my horizons, seeing more than one road to God. We wanted our children to grow up with a sense of religious community. Eventually, we selected Gillis's childhood religion for the church that we would attend as a family. Then I became the convert to his denomination.

Over the course of decades, the childhood roots of my religious upbringing dissipated. When I was examining the façade of my career and how important an identity it was to me, I knew I also had to re-examine religion. Strike that. I needed to re-examine spirituality.

I re-read some journal entries. When I had written my five-page anger epistle in the midst of my deep depression, I realized I blamed God when Gillis was injured and unable to work for several years. I blamed God for making me a working mother who could not stay home with her children. How could I believe in a God like that? I wanted to believe in a God of love. I also wanted to believe in a spiritual, natural force in alignment with my experience and objective evidence.

I wanted to put my spirituality into perspective. I wanted to focus on what I had developed as my own spiritual belief system outside the bounds of doctrine. I wanted to make sense out of the fragments that I had glommed together over the years and re-examine the pieces from childhood that stuck to me in unconscious ways. I journaled about lingering beliefs. I tried them on, researched them, and read a variety of viewpoints. I realized that although I initially had detached from the religion itself out of antagonism, I no longer held anger toward it.

I now had my own way of thinking and followed my internal compass. I wrote down my own tenets. Part of this is a belief in connectedness. We are human, and we are nature. Nature has good and bad. Each person has good and bad in them. I have good and bad in me. I take all of it. I wrap myself in it and acknowledge that I have all these aspects to myself, and it doesn't require me to judge myself in the same way I had in the past. It only needs me to love and have an open heart that will hold appropriate boundaries and provide self-love so I may care for others. I now use regular meditation practices as a way to maintain a sense of connectedness and draw from the well of inspiration that springs from it.

I decided if new information surfaces as I evolve and grow, my spiritual dimension could also expand and morph.

Whispers

Floating gently down
the streaming flow

Wondering which bend
or fork I'll go

So many paths
in my mind's eye

Nature has wisdom,
master plans by and by

Gentle oar dipping
on occasion to steer

Allow the unfolding
divine whispers hear

Higher Power

In my heart space,
Spirit guides,
Providing courage and
Strength besides.

Tapping my passion,
Intuition and love,

Bringing healing and peace
From above.

May I always
Feel your presence,
My Higher Power and
Spiritual essence.

Through meditation, I gained inspiration and intuitive
guidance. The voice of my inner peace was preparing to unleash a
shockwave that would reverberate with lasting healing.

ಬಂಆ

It is late 2015, and I have finished writing my first manuscript of
this book. Yet, I now feel prompted to write one more section.
Sensing it will require both deep forgiveness and transcendent
reconciliation, I close my eyes and let my deft fingers type. I turn
my attention to an early childhood memory my conscious mind
has never before allowed to surface.

My heart pounds in my constricted throat. My breathing
shallows. I swallow hard the acrid spittle and plummet into
palpable fear as I pierce nearly five decades of psychological
protection. I peer into my mind's grimmest gloom, ready to
exhume the ghoul, and brace for Beth's bombshell.

LEANING LEFT

I will turn left and walk a new path...

21

NEFARIOUS NEIGHBOR

I am hiding in my closet, my new Beth cave,

a safe haven from my tormentor...

∞ 1967 ∞

In my memory, the house looms charcoal gray, though that's not the actual color. Jutting gables emerge unshrouded from my mind's oppressive murky mist. Sensing the gloom and dreariness the recollection evokes in me, I brand the building with one word—sinister.

As I think of myself as a little girl on that day, the impression is both powerful and frightening. That child doesn't want to remember the episode that started her down the path that shut the door on Beth some years later as a teenager, but my adult self will guide her.

Surfacing the memory gives me shivers, and eerie tingles pulsate throughout my entire body even now, as I write the words. I am actually terrified as I allow the event's emotions to envelop me.

I am in first grade. I picture myself with my short, pixie-style haircut, wearing my purple dress with white polka dots. My sockless feet, wearing white plastic sandals, are crossing our driveway. The sun has touched my hair, weaving honey-colored highlights throughout my straight, dark brown strands. It has also kissed my nose, leaving sprinkles of tan freckles across my bridge and a constant rosy pink burn at its tip. The side yard is dotted with a multitude of bright-orange poppies with black centers. I walk down the sidewalk, as I have so many other days, to arrive at my neighbor's house.

In my mind's eye, I see the neighbor's black door in front of me. Before we open the door to this memory, I decide I will visualize taking young Beth by the hand, and together with my fully mature Elizabeth self, my young Beth self will explore and revisit what has scared her for so long. Beth feels at ease now so that she can describe what is happening.

I live in a small town where nobody worries about locking their doors. It is normal for me to visit adults in my neighborhood. There are very few children to play with, and I easily make friends with people of all ages. I have even become good friends with the university student across the street. She has shown me how she plays the acoustic guitar, and we have a lot of fun singing together.

I am not at the student's house now. I am at another home that I visit. I see my neighbor in her large, Victorian-style kitchen as its dill aroma wafts my way. She is wearing a long, black dress that ends near her ankles. She always wears a black dress, black stockings, and black shoes now, representing her mourning as a widow. Her long, silvery white hair forms a neat knot at the nape of her neck. Her face is creased with wrinkles that show her smile lines even when she is relaxed. When I think of her, it is a happy sensation. I enjoy helping her in the kitchen.

She has left the kitchen now, and today I do not immediately leave the house. One of her adult sons, a man of about forty, has promised to show me something. I am to follow him up the stairs.

A long, dark-brown wood banister stretches along the outside of the staircase. The steps are made of the same stained wood, but carpeting covers most of the tread. As we climb the stairs in spooky silence, I grip the image of my older self until the knuckles of my right hand turn white. The fingertips of my left hand glide innocently along the banister.

I see the man who is my neighbor at the top of the stairs, coaxing me to come to him. He is waiting with his arms crossed impatiently. He has jet-black hair and a tanned olive complexion with a mustache. He is wearing a white shirt and black pants. I obey him and continue walking up the stairs. I am curious about his surprise.

His bedroom has a large, walnut-colored armoire against the left side of the wall, with a chair next to it in the corner. I imagine my adult self, standing at the corner near the chair, lending moral support to my child self as the scene unfolds. To the right, he has a tall poster bed where the posts are higher at the headboard and lower at the footboard. He has not put me on the bed, however.

He tells me, "This is a special sharing time that we need to keep secret."

I agree, eager to see what he wants to share with me. I am standing at the foot of the bed. Beneath my feet, a large, oval, multi-colored braided rug covers the floor—similar to the kind my paternal grandmother used to make from rags. He has dark-brown eyes. The smile is gone from them. His hands are big, with a brownish tinge and thick, black hair.

He takes down his pants, and I see his white underwear. He shows me something weird and ugly. He wants me to play with it. I don't want to touch it. Something feels wrong. He urges me to take off my own white panties. He has shown me "his" and now I'm supposed to show him "mine." I stand frozen. I don't like this kind of sharing, but I don't know what else to do.

He is irritated at my hesitation and decides to take over. I am lying on the multi-colored braided rug now. He pins down my body. He covers my mouth. I am screaming, but the cries are all inside my head because my throat constricts and strangles the sound. Warm tears stream in silence down the side of my face and drown in my damp hair. I feel utterly helpless. I am not entirely sure what is happening, but I know it does *not* feel right.

The bedroom has photos of his father and mother on the dresser in wide, wooden frames. I look at their faces suspended in time, as panic and terror wash over me. I nestle a secret hope in my heart that they will come to my rescue, although I know the father cannot, because he is no longer alive.

In fact, his mother unwittingly comes to my rescue. His mother calls to him; she calls *for* him. It distracts him as he attempts to answer her. His pants hang scrunched around his ankles, and that ugly thing, now stiff, hangs over me.

He hobbles to the dark wooden door, opens it, and calls back to answer. He stands to the side, clutching the ornate oval handle with his hand, using the door to shield his partially naked body from the narrow opening while holding his sagging trousers and underwear with his other hand. He wedges his head in the doorway gap. It seems wide enough for my six-year-old body. In that instant, I seize my opportunity for escape. I jump up from the rug, squeeze past him before he can grab me, and charge down the long staircase.

I leave my white panties behind where he has discarded them. I have no time to retrieve them. I dash out the front door and down the sidewalk to my house, my sanctuary. I sprint up my own staircase and race to the right, into my bedroom. I pull my knees to my chest, using the skirt of my purple-and-white polka-dot dress to cover my legs and my nakedness. I interlock my arms around my knees and begin to rock back and forth. I erupt in sobbing shrieks punctuated by the broken breaths of my spastic, heaving chest. I don't quite know what has happened, but it feels so terrible. I feel so terrible.

White, diamond-shaped wood is a lattice for my bedroom windows. The windows open to a red-tiled porch roof we sometimes climb to look at stars or fireworks. It provides a beautiful bird's-eye view of the neighborhood.

My thoughts are not about that latticed window today. My thoughts are not about the twin bunk beds I share with my older sister. My thoughts are about what just happened to me.

I am hiding in my closet, my new Beth cave, a safe haven from my tormentor.

In that moment, I swear to myself that I will never abandon my children and will not be a working mother while they are young. I will be home to protect my children from such predators. Of course, as a child, I don't have this conscious thought that my neighbor is a *predator*, but I know what he has done is vile. The trauma sends tremors of pain and shame through me.

At the same time, I decide that when I do finally work, it will be part time so that I will be home to meet my children after school. I also proclaim that I will be a nurse and will heal and help people. I need to heal. I want to care for my aching agony. Maybe if I help other people heal, it will help me mend too.

I remember that my neighbor has told me we should keep this special sharing time between us a secret. I know this secret is not a good one, but the way it makes me feel is so disgraceful and dirty that it makes me feel sinful.

I don't want to feel like I have done something wrong. I want to be the perfect princess, keeping the illusion of the obedient child that earns Mom and Dad's love. I like that image, and I don't want to destroy that imagery in their minds. I can never tell them. I will never tell anyone. It is a horrendous, filthy secret to entomb in that closet, my Beth cave.

80CB

In the weeks that pass, I begin wetting my bed at night. Mom never makes a big deal about it. I'm child number six, so she knows accidents happen. She gives me a towel to put on the sheet so I can go back to sleep. I don't connect this to my recent trauma. It's simply one more thing spreading me in shame, though.

One day in school, paralysis seizes my limbs. My psyche slithers away from the classroom. I cannot raise my hand to get the hall pass for the lavatory. I sit motionless as if pinned by an unseen force. I have no choice but to release the warm urine as it floods the seat beneath me and the same purple-and-white polka-dot dress. Shame streams from my chest, flushing my cheeks. I feel the whole class must be watching me. How do I excuse myself from this without getting embarrassed?

I wait until all the other children have left the room for recess. I see the expression in my kind teacher's eyes. She doesn't judge me harshly, not as critically as I do myself. I am ushered to the office where the school secretary tells me I can go home and get a change of clothes. I am both humiliated and relieved.

I don't know at the time these incidents are merely one way of reacting to what has happened to me. I only know the shame that I am not in control of my body during the day and night.

I shove that special sharing secret into the fracture within my heart and bury its remains in the new cave. I vow, in my immature mind, that this monster will not haunt me again. I believe if I wish it away, like in the fairy tales, it will make it so. I wish for some magical power to grant this release.

My defenses inter more than the memory of my neighbor's nasty surprise. Shards of my spirit also sever my utmost aspiration and entomb it in Beth's catacomb.

My budding passion to be a writer is dead.

ᛒ 2015 ᚳ

That was the inception of Liz. That incident in 1967 lay undisturbed until it was stirred at age thirteen. I buried the conscious memory of it fathoms deep. My teenage trauma triggered Beth squarely into the closet, her imaginary cave, stuffing emotions one by one into an enormous lake and building an imaginary ice barrier against feeling the anguish.

I also connect the dots and understand why, when I am angry or feel victimized, my throat constricts, and it provokes profound pain. I always want to cry. No wonder. I couldn't scream out when I was six. The circumstances differ, but the emotions from that event affect me similarly.

Beth's trauma is the primary reason I had wanted to be a mother who stays at home with her children. This was the reason my depression and feelings of guilt over being a working mother were intense and irrational. I not only believed I had failed my children, but I had also failed my child self.

During my deep depression, I finally was unconsciously processing the unrecognized anger of that long-ago childhood betrayal. Of course, I was also working through other issues. This event felt foundational—the cornerstone.

My utmost passion could not be fully uncovered until I allowed myself to remember why I had buried it when I was six.

I Set We Free

From shadows past,
I see you, faceless, beckoning.
I set you free.

My body shakes with terror,
Nefarious game you play.
I set me free.

I buried you along with me
and my emotional vulnerability.
I set we free.

No more haunting.
No more secrets.
No more shame.

I choose to live among the light.
I set you free.
I set me free.
I set we free.

22
ELIZABETH EMERGES

Rebirthing has begun...

The gift to me is that this trauma from my childhood is healing after remaining buried and sealed in that imaginary cave. I have unconsciously been unwinding this by exploring my shadow, forgiving myself, and tapping into the passion I denied and buried that day in the closet.

I appreciate that the understanding of this incident has come as an adult when I can extend compassion to myself. My journey of self-discovery and renewal has been able to lessen the guilt and shame of *all* my actions and experiences over the years. I am grateful that I have the capacity to forgive my perpetrator (now deceased) for this particular assault and myself for its aftermath.

I share my experience and the healing it brings because everyone has some sort of ordeal causing great distress. Whatever trauma you have gone through, the circumstances of the actual event are not as important as how you *feel* about the incident. If it makes you feel less than, inadequate, shameful, guilty, enraged, or any other intense emotion, then something needs to heal. I urge you to take the time to allow yourself compassion. Take steps to recover from the story that plays in your mind as you relive the events or shut yourself off from the past.

Everything that happens to us provides an opportunity for learning and healing. I buried my experience only to resurrect it when I could handle it. I pray you have the strength to revisit whatever you need to face whenever you are ready.

I looked at my poem, "From the Shadows." I cried after I had changed my punctuation and spacing to make it clear what I meant. I re-read it. What struck me, what made me cry, was not sorrow. It was joy. It was the statement that rebirthing has begun. I can fully acknowledge and embrace the passion for writing that I have hidden from myself for forty-eight years.

When the doors continued to close on human resources jobs and contracts, I now know it was because my soul was looking to resurrect something profound. My last piece of resistance to shedding my human resources identity melted away in a meditative moment I transcribed:

Excerpt Nineteen

The gentle breeze whispers in my ear, this is your destiny. You are an author, and nearly every day you need to write. For this is your soul speaking. You cannot hear it as but just the faintest of whispers at this time, but you know that this resonates with you. You don't know what your voice is telling you in this moment because you have not learned yet to trust it with the rest of your life, but you will.

This is the softer message that I give you today, Elizabeth. You are whole. You are one. You are divine, and you will do this for the rest of your life.

You're getting your balance right now, and you will find it very solidly. You must trust yourself, and you are seeing the beginnings of this. It will only become stronger as you resist less and give in to the divine—to allow it to guide you, and allow yourself to trust in something that you are a part of that is bigger than you and yet is part of you.

You will learn so much more than you ever thought possible, and you will be in the comfort of the spirit that is divine, eternal, unchanging, and all-knowing—with the natural aspect of the spirituality that your soul has been searching for all these decades, ever since you left your childhood religion.

This is the message that kept you awake yesterday and today. You needed to allow it to come through. You were right that you had a certain excitement that couldn't be contained in your body. You got that message in your solar plexus. It serves you to be anxious, and it serves you to be excited. This is the excitement of your soul awakening.

You are in metamorphosis, and you are extremely excited about this on a conscious and unconscious level. You have so much that you want to do, give, be, and you aren't sure yet how this will happen. Yet as you trust and walk forward, the path will be shown to you.

You are following what you need to right now. You are on course. Continue the connection with your divine, the divine that is us all, and within us all. Let this be your guide.

This is the relationship that is in rebirth…your relationship with yourself. The old is dying. You are rebirthing a new relationship with yourself.

My conversation a few years prior surges through my mind.

"Gillis, remember when you asked me if I was going to quit my job and become a writer? I said, 'Of course not. That would be crazy.' Well, now I'm telling you, I'm not a human resources person anymore. I'm a writer."

Gillis's ebony face flashes his broad, ivory smile as he says, "Go for it, hon."

৪৩৩

I now venture along the new way my nocturnal messages revealed to me.

I have surrendered to the view that my career, my HR-ness, is not the full encapsulation of my professional identity. The wizard of my dream was prophetic. The good died, making way for the great. I am in a transformation still unfolding.

From the depths of my despair, my childhood passion began to emerge as I scribbled my torment, allowed expression of my emotions, and shaped them into the poems I share with you today. I wrote about my anguish and conflict in many different ways: through poetry, journaling, responding to exercises in books, and linking these pieces together in the narrative you're reading.

I bundled all the seedlings and branches to share with you the journey I went through, while I was going through it. You have these trees as guideposts in this forest. It's only now I *can* knowingly link them as a forest.

My wish is that my story has imbued a measure of hope within you. These journeys are never finished. I'm a work in progress and always will be. And so will you. That's the point. It's the journey—not the destination. We all are on similar voyages. We search and find meaning. We experience joy and sorrow. We dance in the duality.

Meaning is *uncovered.* Meaning is within, and it is personal. My meaning need not be anyone else's. Your meaning need not be someone else's. Meaning for me is about the relationship with self, a connection to others, and a limitless journey of development. It took time to discover.

My journey will be a lifetime of striving to be a better, more loving self to me—while learning, growing, and sharing my experiences, insights, and talents with others who are interested. It's part of writing my story. While sharing, I won't carry the pillow with you, but I'm happy to coach you. You're responsible for holding your own pillow.

Here is the song of my journey so far. It first came to me as the refrain, "and so it changed my life." The original melody lingered long enough for me to capture it before I fully awoke.

The words and tune didn't come all at once. The words came to me over a period of several months as I explored inner thoughts and beliefs about myself. The tune is not finished. The lyrics may not be finished either, just as my journey is not finished. My wish is that you find, through whatever resources available to you, the power to change your life in a way meaningful to you.

Changed My Life

Didn't allow the feelings to be felt
Stuffed inside the closet
Emotional skeletons
Too much baggage overwhelmt

Peeking out only now and then
When logic and pragmatism overrun
Only to be hidden away again

Spock-ish style works fine you see
No need to change my life
Change my life

Raging waters bursting intensity
No floodgates to control
Submerged in woeful emotionality
As far as the eye could see

Went through the valley of my shadow
And wished for death
Just an everlasting sleep
That would bed my last breath

A specter feasting on my every flaw
Don't want to live this life
Live this life

Reaction junkie addicted to helping you
Obsessed with finding solutions to
Your problems you didn't ask me do
So your burden became mine too

Resentful you didn't appreciate
Efforts in rescuing capable you
Leaving disempowering residue

Key is I'm responsible just for me
And so it changed my life
Changed my life

Unravel repetitive compulsion
Bindings to set me free
From the enmeshing dance of
Dysfunctional codependency

How could I know the pain I hid
Repressing anger inside, stole
Joy, too, crushing spirit under its lid?

Uncovered and followed my passions
And so it changed my life
Changed my life!

23
EPILOGUE

I feel whole and healed...

I am walking in the hills, through the lush, emerald green vegetation of the place I envision during my meditative moments. The wind whispers among the leaves, as the breeze gently brushes my long, wavy blonde hair past my cheek. Today, I do not imagine myself turning right as I always do. I will turn left and walk a new path that I have not taken before in my visualizations.

I stroll to my imaginary place of inspiration. I rest in the circle of light in the crimson sandstone cavern of my thought. Because I feel whole and healed, I need the shelter of a cave no more. I imagine my old Beth cave is now open. It has expanded into an Elizabeth enclave. The roof is gone, and the walls have moved backward into a natural mountain.

The red, orange, and brown shades of its sandstone face are magnificent, like Zion National Park. I crane my long, slender neck and look up at the lofty, distant, natural wall. I no longer need nearby barriers for protection. Its stunning face offers splendor and majesty. My blue-green eyes behold its beauty.

I look around and then wonder how magnificent this view must be at night. I imagine stars twinkling and blinking in the sky. The Milky Way is laden with thousands of shiny lights dotting the darkness. I feel like I am made of star stuff, as Carl Sagan would say. We are all part of the same star stuff. We are all connected.

I love the idea that I link to everything and everyone all at the same time. I embrace the infinite—both infinitesimal and immeasurable—like opulent galaxies barely fitting into our comprehension. Clearly, there is much beyond our current understanding. This journey may never finish. When I am gone… perhaps then will I know.

When I Am Gone (Re-visioned)

When I am gone
No more will I be
In this world

I join in the universe
I join with
the dust of my ancestors
I join with
the rest of the star stuff
in the heavenly galaxy

When I am gone
It will be perfect
as many say
It will be perfect
because I am nature

Nature is in me
Nature is me
Nature is we

Your loving journey companion,

Elizabeth

REFLECT AND RESPOND

You wondered if my story might help you. Then, you finished reading the book—that already demonstrates your determination. Now, it's your turn to help yourself. Before you begin, know this. You are capable. You are more capable than you imagine right now.

These pages summarize key points from each chapter, pose questions, and offer suggestions. Take time to reflect and write your responses to them.

As you work through each section, be gentle on yourself. Don't rush through the questions in one sitting. Give yourself some time. And don't go through this process alone. Reach out to others. I shared my insights and anxieties with an intimate network of family and friends as well as a coach. In addition to opening up to your loved ones, use the help of a professional counselor or coach when possible.

Hopeless Hole

Depression felt like a whirlpool sucking me into the abyss of a black hole, sapping all my hope. Everyday actions seemed like slogging through quicksand.

We each have a point when we hit rock bottom. We also have our own ways of experiencing despair.

- What does depression feel like for you?
- Describe the time you hit your lowest point. If depicting that moment in the first person is too distressing, consider writing it in the third person.

Angry Acknowledgment

I learned that suppressing my anger contributed to depression.
Anger offers cues about infringed boundaries. It also motivates us to act. Examine your own anger-depression connection.

- What are you angry about?
  Start by writing *I am most angry that...*
- Are you able to express your anger responsibly?
- What are your self-imposed anger myths?
- How would you rewrite them?

Roots of Rumination

My negative self-talk branded me as a bad mother.
Our minds mull over and obsess about the past, replaying messages of why we should believe ourselves to be inadequate.

- What are the roots of your rumination?

Passionate Pursuits

Suppressing anger also stifled my ability to acknowledge the passion I felt about my career.

- What are a few things you most enjoy or feel passionate about?
- When did you last do them?

Poetic Parturition

In struggling to cultivate a new relationship with myself, I unwrapped the creative gift of poetry. It allowed me to express both artistry and emotion.

- What could be a silver lining in your dark cloud of depression?

Chawing Chatter

I call my critical chatterbox the propagandizer.

We all have scathing self-talk, but when we're depressed, the tirade can seem overwhelming.

• What name would you like to give your inner critic?

Flipping Failure Focus

I took fears from the shadows by acknowledging and examining them. It weakened their power over me.

If you name, describe, and begin to recognize fears, they will lessen their grip on you.

• What is the word association you have with failure? Write down the first word to pop in your mind.
• How does it make you feel?
• What is the sensation in your body?
• How can you shift perspective to see that a failed situation or event does not define your worth?

Parasitic Problem

I had not uncovered meaning nor pursued dreams that were uniquely mine. I attached myself to my family's ambitions and absorbed vicarious meaning through them.

• Finish the following sentence, and write all the ideas that come to mind:
    If I only needed my imagination to create a life full of meaning, I would...

Beth's Betrayal

Although I believed I had earlier dealt with my teenage trauma, it left an unacknowledged residual influence into adulthood. I began processing through it at a much deeper level.

Dancing with Darkness

My internal propaganda of shame and guilt caused me to question my ability to make decisions and handle what would come my way in the future.

Imagine the relief you would feel if you faced and embraced all aspects of yourself without condemnation.

- Do you trust yourself?
- If not, why not?
- How can you regain self-trust?

Beginning to Blend

I traced back to childhood memories until I remembered the first time I stashed secrets. Then I confronted them with exercises from self-help books. Meditation and nature reinforced my emergent healing.

- Imagine a location—a natural setting—where your mind relaxes and heart opens. This spot is your own unique place of inspiration and connection.

- Consider taking a mental mini-vacation with a guided meditation. Read the poems again on pages 106-107 to get started.

Meaningful Mentor

In my ongoing search for passion and meaning, I discovered that helping people learn and grow wasn't just an ability. It was a gift planted in me long ago by a nurturing mentor. Meaning was beginning to replace the void.

- Who do you most value as your mentor?
- Consider sending a thank-you note to him or her.

Unemployment Unease

When I no longer had a job to define me, I searched for my authentic identity. Although I grappled with bouts of hopelessness, I used this period to work on my self-development.

Rejection Connection

Instead of wallowing in despair, I submerged in and expressed my outrage. It served as a catalyst to begin broadening my professional pursuits.

Addiction Awareness

After uncovering I am a codependent rescuer—a compulsion as damaging as any other addiction—I realized self-development is not a one-time experience; it's a way of life.

The many months of emotional exercise paid off. I finally uncovered my priceless passion: writing.

Deltoid Dysfunction

I gained awareness about dysfunctional interpersonal dynamics explained by the Karpman Drama Triangle. I began to step away from that whirlwind's power over me.

- Think of an upsetting interaction where you played in the Drama Triangle. Who were in which roles?
- How could you have responded differently instead of joining the game?

Gratitude with Attitude

Through a daily search for gratitude, I surrendered to my family's situation. Then the circumstances began to shift.

- Begin your own daily gratitude with attitude log.
  Today, I am grateful for…

Compassionate Companion

Through self-forgiveness practices, I determined that everything is an opportunity to learn and grow. I found genuine compassion for myself and the treasure of sparkling self-love.

Divine Devotion

I re-examined traces from my childhood religious tenets. Then, I documented my current belief system and sources of inspiration. I became better at receiving insights.

- What are your personal spiritual beliefs or inspirational sources?
- Take deep breaths, calm your mind, and draw your own inspiration. Allow the voice of your own truth, as you understand it, to speak.

Nefarious Neighbor

I remembered my most traumatic childhood incident after having repressed it for nearly five decades. All the puzzle pieces from my life clicked into place. My picture was complete.

Elizabeth Emerges

Through a journey of self-discovery and renewal, I replaced self-loathing with lasting self-love and habitual happiness.

You can, too.

INDEX OF POEMS